WILLIAM LILLY'S HISTORY
OF HIS LIFE AND TIMES

WILLIAM LILLY'S HISTORY OF HIS LIFE AND TIMES

FROM THE YEAR 1602 TO 1681

* * * * *

Written by Himself
IN THE SIXTY-SIXTH YEAR OF HIS AGE
TO HIS WORTHY FRIEND
ELIAS ASHMOLE, ESQ.

* * * * *

PUBLISHED FROM THE ORIGINAL MS.
LONDON, 1715

* * * * *

300TH ANNIVERSARY EDITION
OF THE ORIGINAL PRINT
PUBLICATION

* * * * *

Introduced & Annotated by
WADE CAVES
With a Foreword by Philip Graves

* * * * *

PUBLISHED BY RUBEDO PRESS
AUCKLAND · SEATTLE
MMXV

© Rubedo Press 2015. All rights reserved.
With the exclusion of the public domain text,
no part of this work may be reproduced without
express permission from the publisher. Brief passages
may be cited by way of criticism, scholarship, or review,
as long as full acknowledgement is given.

William Lilly's History
of his Life and Times:
From 1602–1681
By William Lilly
Edited by Elias Ashmole
Introduction and Annotations by Wade Caves
Foreword by Philip Graves

Published by Rubedo Press
220 2nd Ave S #91
Seattle WA 98104
WWW.RUBEDO.PRESS

ISBN: 978-1-943710-04-1

Design and typography
by Aaron Cheak

TABLE OF CONTENTS

Acknowledgements, *vii*

Foreword, by *Philip Graves, ix*

Introduction, by *Wade Caves, xvii*

Advertisement, 1

William Lilly's History of His Life and Times, 7

Epitaphs, 182

Butler's Character of William Lilly, 188

Bibliography, 193

List of Figures

Event Chart for the Coronation of Charles I, *xix*
Horary Chart for the Strength of the Presbytary Party, *xxiv*
Event Chart for the Execution of Charles I, *xxx*
Horary Chart: 'If King Charles should bee beheaded', *xxxii*
The Saturn-Jupiter Opposition of 1653, *xxxvi*

List of Plates

Plate 1. William Lilly, *facing title*

Plate 2. William Lilly, 6

Plate 3. Dr. Simon Forman, 31

Plate 4. John Booker, 57

Plate 5. Charles the Second, 75

Plate 6. Charles the First, 83

Plate 7. Hugh Peters, 103

Plate 8. Speaker Lenthal, 123

Plate 9. Oliver Cromwell, 133

Plate 10. Dr. John Dee, 163

Plate 11. Edward Kelly, 167

Plate 12. Napier of Merchiston, 171

ACKNOWLEDGEMENTS

I extend the deepest gratitude to Jenn Zahrt and Aaron Cheak, my representatives at Rubedo Press, whose tireless commitment to the project cuts through in its final form. To Eric Purdue, who graciously assisted in translating some of the more puzzling Latin passages included in the source material; any errors that remain are my own. And to the industrious Philip Graves, for his willingness to review the annotated material and provide moving insights as an astrological historian.

With great thanks to Paul Kiernan, one of my closest confidants and friends, whose advice along the way has been invaluable. To all of my astrological friends who encouraged me to publish, and were as eager as I was to see this material come to life. And to Jeremy Biglow, for his endless supply of moral support.

A special note of gratitude to my mentor and treasured friend, Deborah Houlding, under whose careful instruction I continue to grow. Her selfless guidance enables my relationship with astrology to deepen, and I find myself learning new ways to appreciate the subtle beauties and mysteries of the Natural World as a result.

Finally, to Mr. William Lilly himself, England's own Merlin, whose contributions to the field of astrology have inspired thousands upon thousands to take up the art and make the most of the years we have here on this earth. *Ars longa, vita breva.*

FOREWORD

THE PRESENT WORK IS A NEWLY ANNOTATED EDITION OF THE autobiography of a seventeenth-century astrologer: not just any seventeenth-century astrologer of moderate renown, but singularly the most influential astrologer to have written in English at any point in history. For both within his time and in the modern era, William Lilly (1602–1681) stands without peer. His extraordinary degree of influence can be seen in three key respects: his composition of astrological texts in English, the enduring popularity of his work, and his unparalleled access to the highest levels of power in British society.

Lilly was the chief pioneer and instigator in the line of substantive astrological writing in the vernacular tongue of the people of Great Britain. His main work, *Christian Astrology Modestly Treated of in Three Books* (1647; reprinted 1659), extending to approximately 875 pages of printed matter, was the first general and reasonably comprehensive instructive manual on the theory and practice of astrology to be authored in the English language, covering as it does the fundamentals of astrology, rules for horary judgements and rules for the judgement of nativities. Prior to its appearance, a detailed knowledge of astrology was almost exclusively the preserve of those with a command of Latin; and the study and practice of astrology had consequently largely been limited to the privileged gentlemanly and scholarly classes in early seventeenth-century Britain.

Despite his father's eventual decline into poverty which denied Lilly the possibility of attending university, Lilly was privately tutored in Latin in his youth, and developed a spoken and written proficiency that far surpassed that of his peers. Lilly's study of Latin would greatly benefit him only a few short years on. In his early thirties, when he acquired sufficient interest and opportunity to learn astrology, Lilly was able to read and thoroughly understand all of the extant Latin treatises and manuscripts on astrology that were available to him in England. He then took it upon himself to selectively filter, synthesise, and correct their teachings. This labour was distilled into the component parts of *Christian Astrology*, a work he frequently refers to in his autobiography as his "Introduction."

Prior to 1647, the only noteworthy printed treatise of astrology originally written in English was *A Treatise of Mathematicall Phisicke*, penned by a G. C. gent. Practicioner in Phisicke. This treatise, limited in its focus to medical astrology, fills barely seventy pages and was not published as an independent work. Rather, it was tacked on to the second edition (1598, after the first of 1583) of the English translation by Fabian Withers of sixteenth-century French astrologer Claude Dariot's popular work, *A Brief and most easie Introduction to the Astrological Judgement of the Starres*.

In a separate, shorter work entitled *Anima Astrologiae, or A Guide for Astrologers* (1676), Lilly also translated into English excerpts from the Latin writings of medieval Italian astrologer Guido Bonatti and sixteenth-century Italian astrologer Girolamo Cardano (Jerome Cardan). Lilly composed numerous other brief works in English, chiefly prophetic tracts on current political and military matters in Britain, that were met with great public interest. Some of these courted considerable controversy, to the extent that Lilly was hauled up for hearings on more than one occasion to defend charges brought against him by both political and religious adversaries.

The combined impact of his major and minor astrological works in English was the engineering of a heightened popular interest in astrology that would endure in Britain throughout the rest of the seventeenth century, even while astrology on the European continent sank into a deep decline from which it would not extricate itself for another two centuries. Significant English-language works by Nicholas Culpeper, William Ramesey, John Gadbury, Henry Coley, Richard Saunders, John Middleton, John Partridge, William Salmon, Joseph Blagrave, George Wharton, John Goad, Richard Kirby, and John Bishop, along with others of lesser importance, followed in Lilly's wake between the 1650s and 1690s.

Lilly's writings on astrology have withstood the test of time, proving to be enduringly popular far beyond his death. John Partridge (1644–1714), the last major influential figure among that aforementioned cohort of seventeenth-century English astrologers, suffered the most cruel derision at the hands of popular author and satirist Jonathan Swift in the latter years of his life. Thereafter, the tide seemed to turn definitively against the credibility of astrology in Britain, with the consequence that only one wholly new major work[1] on astrology appeared in English between the

---

[1] The continuing tradition of astrological almanacs is discounted from that label, although they notably became largely anonymous during this period, their titles spuriously being credited to long-dead astrologers of the seventeenth century. The exception was Samuel Penseyre's *New Guide to Astrology*, 1726.

publication of Partridge's last, *Defectio Geniturarum* (1697), and the appearance of the first part of Ebeneezer Sibly's voluminous *Complete Illustration of the Celestial Science of Astrology* in 1784. And yet, when the nineteenth-century English astrological revival started by Sibly gathered pace, Lilly was one of the first astrologers of bygone times to be brought back into print, albeit somewhat after the issue of the first ever English translations from Placido de Titis and Claudius Ptolemy.

To be precise, it was in 1835 that Richard Morrison, a nineteenth-century English astrologer, who wrote under the familiar pen-name Zadkiel, published his own abridged and partly modernised version of Lilly's "Introduction to Astrology," preferring that name to the full original title of *Christian Astrology*. This amended abridgement was then repackaged in 1852 together with Morrison's own succinct works *A Grammar of Astrology* and *Tables for Calculating Nativities* in a combined edition published by H. G. Bohn. Bohn's edition was reprinted in 1860, and subsequently taken over by the publishers George Bell, which put out no fewer than nineteen further reprints between 1870 and 1939.[2] After a lapse of a quarter of a century, later reprints of the Bohn omnibus edition by various other publishers appeared in 1966, 1967, 1972, 1977, 1978, and 1980. Meanwhile, Lilly's *Anima Astrologiae* also enjoyed two major fresh editions on opposite sides of the Atlantic: that of Wm. C. Eldon Serjeant in London, 1886, and that of Coulson Turnbull in San Diego, California, 1918.

Against the background of this remarkably resilient weathering by Lilly's texts of changing tastes in astrological theory and practice through the generations, British horary astrologer

---

2 At least, these are just the ones that can be traced from library records.

Foreword

Olivia Barclay put forth the idea of reprinting the original full text of *Christian Astrology* in the early 1980s. After a limited photocopy-based run was at first privately issued to an inner circle, to a generally positive reception, this plan became a full-fledged reality with the publication of the Regulus (Clive Kavan) facsimile edition of 1985, the first complete edition of Lilly's main work since the printing of 1659. This met with a tremendous reception, and was followed up by Kavan's new edition of *Anima Astrologiae* the next year. Together with Barclay's own dedicated teaching of traditional horary astrology to a select group of intrepid students, these publishing developments were a cornerstone on which the late twentieth-century revival of original English Renaissance astrology texts was founded.

That revival continues to flourish today. Dedicated publishers of traditional astrology texts – like Ascella (originally Deborah Houlding), Ballantrae Reprint (John Ballantrae), Renaissance Astrology (Christopher Warnock), JustUs Associates (Carol Wiggers), and Astrology Classics (the late David Roell) – have brought the works and words of not only Lilly himself but also most of the later seventeenth-century cohort of British astrologers back into the limelight for seekers.

While some of these operations have since ceased, at least two remain active; and an extensively annotated new edition of Ramesey's main work was recently produced by Kim Farnell. Meanwhile, new substantial and highly popular secondary explicatory texts have been also authored by dedicated scholars and students of Renaissance astrology such as J. Lee Lehman, John Frawley, the late Olivia Barclay herself, and Barbara Dunn. Experienced teachers such as Houlding, Lehman, and Sue Ward continue to train students in the traditional art of horary and other Renaissance astrological techniques. Lilly's influence on the study and practice of astrology can thus clearly be seen to be writ large even in the present day, over 350 years after the last printing in his lifetime of his main work, which remains an essential reference text for today's students and practitioners of horary and traditional natal astrology.

As is apparent in the pages of his autobiography, Lilly exerted during his lifetime a degree of influence at the highest levels of English politics and society that no astrologer before, during, or since his time has equalled. Later sections of this autobiography are replete with vivid and colourful anecdotes concerning the ongoing stream of major events in British history through which Lilly lived, a stream of events in which he himself makes cameo appearances at intervals.

Lilly's attitude to his work as an astrologer deserves special comment. As Ann Geneva points out, he is no charlatan but a true believer in the art of astrology, as well as other predictive arts such as crystal-gazing, as a means of conveying divine intention to mortals. And although he rails in his autobiography against the Presbytery as a strict interpretation of Christianity, holding it to be antagonistic to the divine arts, he evinces much sympathy for Puritanism, and comes across as a devout believer in God. It seems reasonable to conclude, then, that the title of his main work, *Christian Astrology*, was no mere ruse to pacify the ecclesiastical authorities of the times. Rather, it was the expression of his sincere belief that astrology and Christianity are natural partners.

Lilly's *History of His Life and Times* was penned in the 1670s on the request of his patron Elias Ashmole, but was not published until 1715, perhaps partly as a consequence of the sensitive nature of the revelations therein having rendered its publication too risky. A reprint appeared in 1721, another edition in 1774, and that of C. Baldwin in 1822. The Baldwin edition is notable for the addition of a set of twelve illustrative portraits of famous individuals in the story, and is the basis for the widely available version annotated here.

The language in the text is dense and in places antiquated and difficult to follow. Wade Caves is to be congratulated for having pursued his fascination with astrological history and understanding the context of Lilly's work to the extent of extensively annotating his autobiography in ways designed to make it clearer and more comprehensible to the modern reader.

In addition to clarifying obscure and archaic language, and offering his own translations of some of the occasional Latin citations in the text, Caves has brought out the social and political context of Lilly's story in extensive and well-researched elucidatory footnotes. He displays a detailed knowledge of previous secondary scholarship on Lilly and his times; but most of the insights presented are the product of his own careful and studious independent research.

A particular feature of the commentary by Caves is the close attention he has paid to astrological charts of relevance to Lilly's text, including Lilly's own nativity. These discussions enrich the commentary in ways that will strongly appeal to practising astrologers. This was originally a private labour of love on his part, and it brings me great pleasure to know that the fruit of his labour is now being shared with the wider community of astrological students and historians.

PHILIP GRAVES
Sweden, June 2015

INTRODUCTION

THE ENTERTAINING NARRATIVE OF WILLIAM LILLY'S LIFE HAS much to teach us about the early stage upon which our modern astrological history is being built. The beauty of Lilly's text lies in his simplicity in language (Lilly said he wrote *Christian Astrology* so that even those of modest understanding could benefit and learn the art) and his now famous chart examples. Still, the true value of Lilly's legacy can only be appreciated with a proper understanding of the times in which he lived. The 1600s were a precarious time for astrologers in English history, the intensity of which cuts through the finer details in Lilly's work and the work of his contemporaries.

Lilly secured a reputation as England's leading astrologer in the midst of the English Civil War, when the tumultuous reign of Charles I brought the institution of monarchy and the question of Parliamentary power into sharp focus.

In the chart set for Charles I's 1626 coronation (figure 1), we can spot signatures of difficulty that would tarnish the memory of his reign.[1] Mars in his detriment on the first house cusp, almuten

---

[1] Christopher Wordsworth, for the Church of England, *The Manner of the Coronation of King Charles the First of England at Westminster, 2 Feb. 1626* (London: Harrison and Sons, 1892), x. The full text in the Latin reads that the King entered before the tenth hour of the day (when ceremonies com-

of the tenth house, can be taken to signify the newly crowned King. An angular yet debilitated Mars describes an ineffective leader at the forefront of power, someone ambitious and stubborn, a victim of his own aggression. Lilly writes that Mars ill-placed denotes "a lover of slaughter and quarrels, murder, thievery, a promoter of sedition... neither fearing God or caring for man, unthankful, treacherous, oppressors."[2]

Placements in this chart implicate the English people as casualties of the King's hostility and reckless manner of governing. Mars puts his temperamental pressure down on the first house which signifies the people in mundane figures, and Mars is in square to first house ruler Venus. The Moon, a natural significator of the public, is applying to a conjunction with a troubled Saturn, domicile ruler of the tenth house, retrograde and peregrine in the sixth house of affliction and servitude. The square between the two benefics underscores the hard circumstances of the people during the King's rule. Jupiter in the first degree of Scorpio rules the most unfortunate houses in the figure, namely the eighth and twelfth, and his square to first-ruler Venus brings miseries, deceit and misinformation, sickness, an excess of taxation, even unnecessary death, to the people of England. In short, the people should hardly expect to prosper under this King's reign.

The chart speaks volumes about the King's future financial troubles. The second house ruler, Mercury, is retrograde and combust in the eleventh house with Saturn squaring the cusp of the second. Saturn rules the eleventh in the coronation figure,

---

menced), and exited after three o'clock that afternoon.
2 William Lilly, *Christian Astrology* (1647; repr. London: Regulus, 1985), 66. Hereafter *CA*.

Introduction

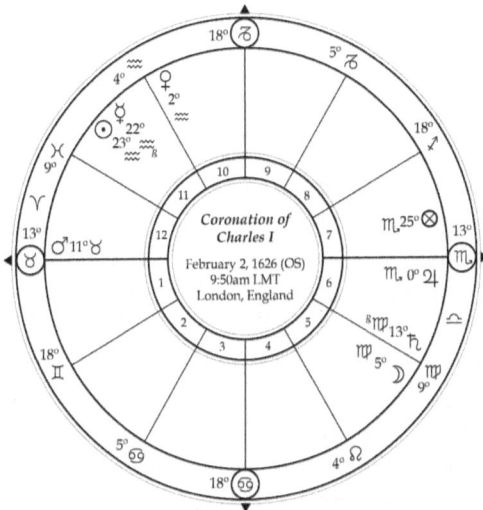

Fig. 1. Event Chart for the Coronation of Charles I

showing contentions with Parliament in passing acts aimed to generate tax revenue.

At this point in English history, Parliament was not yet a permanently standing legislative body. A Parliament was called at the discretion of the Crown, typically for the purposes of carrying out some demand of the King (most frequently for raising tax revenues). Cooperation between Parliament and the Crown created a check and balance system where kings were restrained from excessively loosening their subjects' purse strings. While it may not have directly benefited those English folk in the lower classes who were not yet represented in Parliament, it at least deterred a rapid descent into monarchical tyranny and stayed potential uprisings.

Capricorn on the cusp of the coronation tenth house pulls our attention back to Saturn in square to the second and eighth house cusps. Astrologically this shows that the King's financial fallouts with Parliament are instigated by the affairs of the Crown. Historically, we know this was the case. Being generally obstinate and short-tempered, he decided three years into his reign not to convene Parliament, citing Royal Prerogative, and attempted to rule without a legislative body for over a decade. This period of personal rule from 1629 to 1640 later became known as the Eleven Years' Tyranny, an allusion to the compounding difficulties and tensions that developed during this time.

It had long been Charles I's goal, as it had been his father's, to unite England, Scotland, and Ireland together in one kingdom and one church. This received considerable pushback on religious grounds from the northern kingdoms. During the period of personal rule, Charles I had to get creative with his fundraising, resulting in the re-instatement of unpopular tax acts and ordinances without Parliamentary support. Not surprisingly, the treasury of the Crown still fell short of its financial needs. Charles I found himself requiring support from Parliament to levy taxes and quiet the unrest in the north.

A Parliament was formed in April 1640. The members expressed deep concern over an invasion of Scotland and used their time to air out grievances against the King and his policies. Sensing he was unlikely to garner support for increased tax revenue, Charles I disbanded Parliament a mere three weeks after it had been convened. History would call this assembly the Short Parliament.

Later that year, Charles I would be strong-armed through financial necessity to call another Parliament. Unfortunately for him, this body grew wise to the King's hostilities and took proactive measures. The members passed an act that stated Parliament could only be dissolved with the approval of its members, and another that allowed Parliament to convene every three years with or without the King's consent. The Archbishop of Canterbury, William Laud, who had been selected for the post by King Charles I, was impeached of his seat in Parliament mid-December 1640, as was the King's unwavering supporter John Finch. Accusing both of high treason, the Parliament set out to signal a warning to the King that his manipulation of Parliamentary affairs was at an end. This assembly became known as the Long Parliament, presiding as the legislative body of England from 1640 to 1648, then again from 1658 to 1660, when its members finally voted in favor of dissolution.

But dissolution was many years off, and Charles I was prepared to take drastic steps if it dissipated the political storm that was brewing. In 1642, the King made an attempt to take six members of Parliament by force for their suspected collusion with Scottish rebels. The shortlist included Sir John Hampden, Arthur Hazelrig, Denzil Holles, John Pym, and William Strode from the House of Commons, and Edward Montagu, the second Earl of Manchester, from the House of Lords. Parliament got wind of the plan early enough to act and sent the six away by boat. As he arrived in Parliament, the King quickly realized he was unable to secure the location of those he intended to arrest.

No sovereign had ever attempted such a daring move, and it cost Charles I dearly. His supporters were no longer able to paint him the undeserving victim of disorderly times, and those who were halfhearted in their defiance of the King were now galvanized against him. Parliament poured the army out into the streets and took control of London. Charles I met repeated failures in establishing a safe haven and was forced to flee from the city. Over the next seven years the King would try to regain control of his kingdoms through a successive chain of inadvisable maneuvers, but every step forward seemed to be two steps backward for, in Ebenezer Sibly's words, "this unfortunate monarch."[3]

The social tensions of the time were not only political, but religious as well, and were reflected in the rise of Protestantism in England. The Anglican Episcopal structure placed religious and political power upon appointed bishops, a system that too closely resembled the hierarchy of the Roman Catholic Church. Protestants, particularly the Presbyterian faction, favored a more level ecclesiology, where the Church answered to the State and was restricted in its powers. Perhaps ironically, the Presbytery sought political power to ensure that their agenda retained its strong representation within Parliament. In exchange for military aid, the Long Parliament agreed with the Scottish (who were largely influenced by Presbyterianism) to introduce Protestant reforms in the Church of England. True to their word, the members of Parliament passed an act in 1646 that made the Church subordinate to Parliament, in line with Presbyterian ideals.

Being a resilient bloc in Parliament, Presbyterians enjoyed a great deal of state influence. Nevertheless, the Presbyterians were an austere group and struggled to garner wide public support. Religious and political extremists, they ostracized many conservative members of the Church of England both in and out of Parliament, support they would need to secure their stronghold in English political affairs.

---

3 Ebenezer Sibly, *The New and Complete Illustration of the Celestial Science of Astrology* (London, 1817), 858.

The Presbyterians were also known to take unsavory positions in dealing with an unruly public. Instead of considering complaints from the soldiers about their arrears of pay, for example, the Presbyterians pushed to have them charged and tried as enemies of the state. This highly incensed the New Model Army, and the split between army and Presbytery would only grow more tenuous over time.

The Presbyterians were vocal opponents of astrology, likening it to witchcraft and sorcery. They wielded their political influence to arraign and prosecute practitioners, and even suggested burning astrologers' libraries. Many astrologers became aligned in their opposition to the Presbytery, regardless of their political affiliation. Lilly himself was called to court as a result of Presbyterian complaint more than once, and in his autobiography states why he did not delay in publishing his *Introduction* (known to us as *Christian Astrology*):

> I found it best as unto point of time, because many of the soldiers were wholly for it, and many of the Independent party; and I had abundance of worthy men in the House of Commons, my assured friends, no lovers of Presbytery, which then were in great esteem, and able to protect the art; for should the Presbyterian party have prevailed, as they thought of nothing less than to be Lords of all, I knew well they would have silenced my pen annually, and committed the Introduction unto everlasting silence.

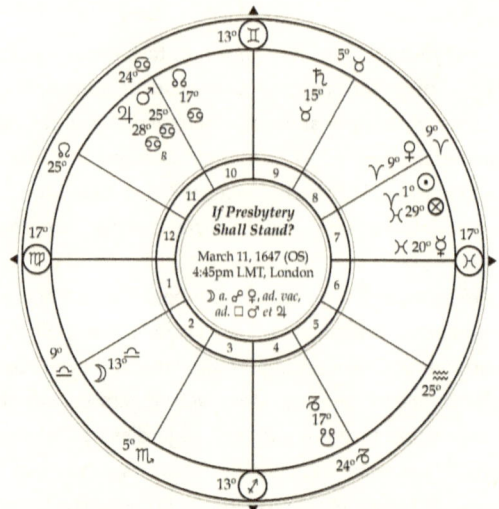

Fig. 2. Horary Chart for the Strength of the Presbytery Party

In 1647, Lilly accepted a query from Sir Thomas Middleton of Chirk Castle who feared the political strength of the Presbyterians.[4] "Seeing they much prevailed," Lilly wrote, "being a member of the House, seriously demanded my judgment, if Presbytery should prevail or not in England?"[5]

This is one of the more subtlety loaded chart judgments Lilly provides in his *Christian Astrology*. Some contemporary astrologers have criticized Lilly for entertaining a horary question for what appears to be a mundane matter. Concerns about radicali-

---

4 Lilly records Middleton being associated with *Chark* Castle, but this is most certainly a misspelling of Chirk, a castle situated on the modern-day northeastern border of Wales and England.

5 *CA*, 439.

ty (i.e., rootedness, appropriateness of subjecting a question to horary) dissipate when we take this question in the context of what was personally at stake for both Lilly and Middleton should the Presbyterians find a permanent stronghold in Britain.

Lilly's judgment in *Christian Astrology* spans a few pages, and it is well worth the time spent dissecting his observations. As the ninth house governs matters of religion, Saturn's position there commands Lilly's immediate attention. Saturn is a slow, immovable planet, the more so when it is placed in earthy, fixed Taurus. It describes the Presbytery as harsh, overbearing, severe, and strict, perhaps too much so for the gentle nature of the English people. Lilly comments that if the Presbyterian leaders loosened their penchant for rigid control, ample opportunity would remain to form a lasting body.

Planets in horary describe the nature of external response, but also shed light on the internal dynamics of the quesited party. When not well dignified, Saturn's placement in a house is a maligning influence that brings covetousness, in-fighting, discontent. Lilly divines from Saturn's position in the ninth that the Presbytery itself will be divided. The young, Lilly writes, are represented by Venus (the ninth house ruler) and the elders by Saturn, each desiring more than they have right to claim.

All significators of the Presbytery in this figure are rendered unfortunate by accidental and essential placements. Venus as ninth-ruler is combust, in the malefic eighth house (twelfth from its own), and in detriment in Aries. Saturn is peregrine, occidental (meaning he sets over the western horizon after the Sun) and lacking affirmative support from fortunate planets in the figure. With cardinal angles, and the majority of planets in cardinal signs, Lilly argues that the Presbyterian grip will not last long. He notices the application from the Moon to the square of Mars, from this judging that the soldiers will rise up to hold the power of the Presbytery in check, and then employs the Moon's immediate application to the square of Jupiter to signify the gentry and those of high clerical office who will stand together to oppose the Presbytery.

Lilly published this judgment in his *Christian Astrology* in 1647. Presbyterians would have seen and had access to his prediction after the text came to publication. It undoubtedly colored the Presbytery's opinion of Lilly, and would be one of many reasons why they found him and his annual almanacs (which Lilly titled *Merlinus Anglicus*, or *The English Merlin*) so particularly dangerous.

Two years after the publication of *Christian Astrology*, in 1649, Presbyterian ecclesiology replaced the traditional Anglican structure and remained in effect for eleven years. Lilly states there was no middle ground between Presbyterian and Independent factions in those years, and the ordinances that the Presbyterians continued to put forward created many enemies. As Lilly predicted, the Presbytery ultimately fell out of favor at the Restoration of monarchy in 1660, and the Church of England assumed much of its former structure and positioning.

Returning to 1647, we find the King falling on hard times. His military forays spelled one disaster after another, resulting in his eventual capture. He was held and heavily guarded in the palace at Hampton Court, and was keen to escape if he could. Lady Jane Whorwood, a Royalist supporter and confidant of Charles I, sought Lilly's astrological guidance on where the King might stay safe and undiscovered. This was a rather bold request, for Lilly made ample space in his almanacs to criticize the affairs of the Crown and the current state of the monarchy in England. Still, Lilly had developed a reputation for assisting those who came in a spirit of sincerity, and he was willing to assist Lady Whorwood if he could. Lilly's judgment pointed to a destination twenty miles northeast where the King could expect safety and secrecy. Whorwood knew of a place in Essex that fit Lilly's description, and the plan for escape was made.

Perhaps unsurprisingly, the King did not trust the counsel of an astrologer who was so vocal against monarchy in the almanacs that flooded the London streets. Instead of repairing to Essex as advised, the King slipped away at nightfall to the Isle of Wight, southwest from London. The plan failed – Parliament was notified of the King's location upon his arrival and sent orders to Colonel Hammond, governor of the Isle of Wight, to detain Charles I and imprison those officers in the King's company. For the next year Hammond would play the *de facto* custodian and jailer of Charles I and his officers.

Lilly advised Whorwood twice more on Charles I's condition, once regarding the potential for escape that required the use of a handsaw. Another produced a day and time to sign terms for his release and return to London, as Parliament was still willing at this stage to negotiate with the King. Charles I failed to heed Lilly's guidance on both accounts, and only aggravated his own situation. Oliver Cromwell, then commander of the New Model Army, had reached his limit in negotiations with the King and refused to parlay further. It was time for decisive action.

In December 1648, Colonel Thomas Pride entered Parliament with a band of soldiers and removed those members of Parliament who either opposed military intervention or wished to continue talks with the Crown. Those MPs who remained after Pride's Purge formed what later became known as the Rump Parliament. (Lilly provided a hilarious anecdote in his autobiography explaining how this Parliament acquired its name: "The citizens took this pulling down of their gates so heinously, that one night the ruder sort of them procured all the rumps of beef, and other baggage, and publickly burnt them in the streets, in derision of the then Parliament, calling them that now sat, The Rump.")

The Rump moved to put King Charles I on trial, setting the commencement date for 20 January 1649. The King refused to plead for the first three days of the trial and challenged the authority of a state court to try a monarch. Unsuccessful in his attempts to halt the proceedings, Charles I was removed from the court at the end of the third day. Witnesses were brought in for the remainder of the trial to testify against the King. Charles I was found guilty and condemned to death by beheading on 26 January (OS). Fifty-nine of the commissioners signed his death warrant, Cromwell the third amongst them.

The execution was scheduled for 30 January. Charles I entered the public arena at 2 PM that day, gave a stirring public speech and was lead to the executioner's block. The whole ordeal was over within the space of fifteen minutes. Sibly, in reference to Charles I's nativity, said,

> This memorable event was effected under the direction of the Part of Fortune to the quartile of the Moon, and the zodiacal parallel of Saturn to the mundane parallel of Mars; and might serve as a useful monitor to succeeding princes, not to trifle with the remonstrances of a free people; nor to hold in defiance that genuine flame of heav-

en-born patriotism, which, when once seriously kindled through an empire, carries all before it, and breaks down every barrier of protection, even to the sacred person of the Lord's anointed.[6]

Though some celebrated the execution of the King (Mrs. John Lisle is on record for saying that "her blood leaped within her to see the tyrant fall"), the beheading of a sovereign shook the emotional core of the English people. Lilly wrote that despite his outspoken stance in favor of Parliament, he retained a deep reverence for monarchy and was disturbed by the result of the King's trial.

In Charles I's execution chart (figure 3, adapted from Sibly's *The New and Complete Illustration of the Celestial Science of Astrology*, 1817), connections are visible not only to the King's nativity, but also to his coronation chart. Transiting Mars, which signified the King in his coronation chart, came to a partile conjunction of the coronation Saturn on the day of his beheading. This conjunction was also in square to transiting Saturn, all disposited by Mercury squaring the coronation ascendant.

This chart also ties in symbolism from another chart that receives very little exposure – a horary that Lilly judged regarding the fatal outcome of Charles I's trial.

Lilly records in his autobiography that he was pained to see Charles I executed. This should not be surprising when we consider that this autobiography was written well after the restoration of monarchy in England. Even Elias Ashmole, in his footnotes on Lilly's autobiography, refers to Charles I as a "martyr."

Even still, it piques my interest as a curious comment given the peripheral accounts available today for contrast.

---

6 Sibly, *Celestial Science of Astrology*, 858.

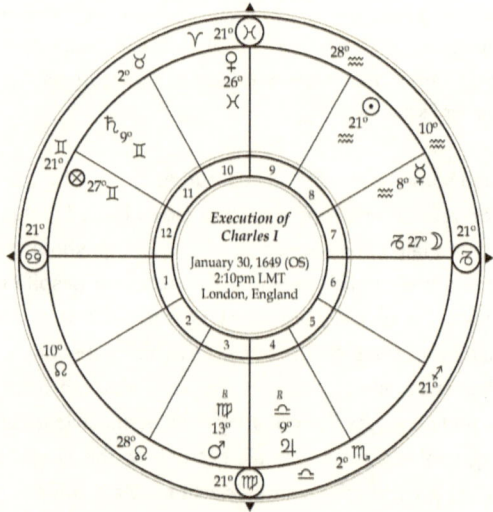

Fig. 3. Event Chart for the Execution of Charles I

We know that only weeks prior, Lilly had been called to a clandestine meeting with Lord Gray (who assisted Colonel Pride in determining who should be removed from Parliament during Pride's Purge) and Hugh Peters. The two requested that Lilly bring two pages from his 1649 almanac. Though not directly stated, it is presumed that the pages they asked for were those for January and February of that year. Evidence is given under January's observations, as Lilly begins, "I am serious, I beg and expect *Justice*..." In his autobiography, Lilly records his hosts' response to that opening line of his monthly predictions:

> "If we are not fools and knaves," saith [Peters], "we shall do justice:" then they whispered. I understood not their

meaning till his Majesty was beheaded. They applied what
I wrote of justice, to be understood of his Majesty, which
was contrary to my intention; for Jupiter, the first day of January, became direct; and Libra is a sign signifying Justice;
I implored for justice generally upon such as had cheated
in their places, being treasurers, and such like officers. I
had not then heard the least intimation of bringing the
King unto trial...

If it seems unlikely that Lilly sat in ignorant silence while the two discussed the trial and potential regicide under hushed voices, his retelling of that meeting becomes even more suspect when one considers a horary judgment published in his *Anglicus, An Ephemeris for 1646 to 1650* – "If King Charles should be beheaded." Dated for 19 January 1649 (OS, 1649 by modern reckoning), this question came to Lilly from a Royalist sympathizer one day before the trial of Charles I commenced. Introducing this judgment, Lilly writes,

There was never in this Kingdom, perhaps in the world, the like Astrological question propounded or answered. A King arraigned in his own Kingdom, his Subjects sitting judges. It is in vain oh Kings of this world to fight against the Decrees of heaven, which have all along seconded this Parliament's proceedings, and have destroyed from the highest to the lowest all those who have opposed them and their Armies.

Lilly's judgment directs us to Jupiter, ruler of the tenth house, and Venus as exaltation ruler of the tenth in Jupiter's terms. These are taken to offer signification of the King. In the figure, Parlia-

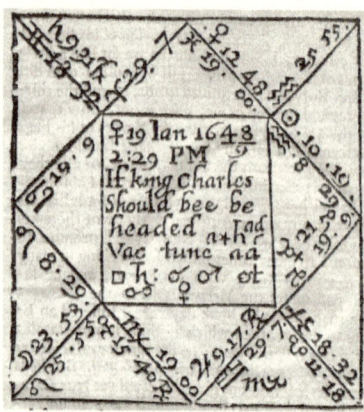

Fig. 4. Horary Chart: 'If King Charles should bee beheaded'

ment is shown by Mercury, ruler of the opposing fourth house, and Mars by virtue of his proximity to the fourth house cusp. Lilly points to the seventh house, tenth from the King's ascendant, to find the judges in the trial, "and therefore Mercury and Saturn do best discover them."

Lilly notes that Jupiter is retrograde and under the earth, in the house of his accusers, "arguing him to be in the power of his enemies and in a sad condition." The generosity between Venus in Pisces and Jupiter in Libra is noted, but as they form no aspect they are not understood to be in reception, which would have undoubtedly aided the King's prospects.

The Moon is situated on the cusp of the third house, conjunct fixed star Regulus (known to bring kings to great heights, but also associated with violence and sudden downfalls) and the King's natal ascendant. The Moon is just entering Saturn's orb by square, the ruler of the radical eighth house of death and the presiding judges. Lilly notes the Moon will then translate the light of Saturn (i.e., the sentence) to the conjunction of Mars, which Lilly connects to both soldier and axe. From Mars, the Moon will move to oppose Venus, co-significator for the King. Venus touches both malefics herself – Saturn by square, Mars by approaching opposition. The case was shut and closed for Lilly – "I certainly concluded, he would die and be put to death."

On His Majesty's behalf, the Royalist querent implored Lilly to look further into the chart to see if the King's life might be spared. Was there some sliver of hope in this chart that might offer some assistance? Turning to the horary, Lilly noted that Jupiter had very recently been in trine to both Sun and Saturn, and that Mercury would perfect a trine with Jupiter in eleven days' time, on 30 January (OS). Upon noting these configurations, Lilly frames his response to the querent: "I said, there would be much intercession for sparing of his life; and that if he escaped the last of January, it was possible he might live a little longer... but God determined his life to end the thirtieth of January."

With all charts exposed, now we can fully appreciate the connections between Charles I's nativity, his coronation chart, the horary figure concerning his death, and his execution chart. The angles of the horary and execution chart are only two degrees separated. These angles also pick up eighth house themes for Charles I. The fourth house cusp in these charts conjunct the King's natal Jupiter at 19° Virgo, who rules his natal eighth house. Jupiter in both horary and execution charts at 9° Libra conjuncts Charles I's natal Moon. The tenth house cusp of the coronation becomes the place of the horary Mercury, which Lilly took to signify the judges who presided over Charles I's trial. This same degree also conjuncts the execution descendent. The Sun, who signifies kings and royalty naturally, is in Aquarius (his detriment) in the coronation, horary, and execution charts, and in two of these charts opposes the King's natal ascendant at 24° Leo. Finally, though this does not complete an exhaustive list of connections, the horary and execution Saturn opposes Charles I's natal Sun at 8° Sagittarius.

Lilly would face the consequences of judging this horary some time after the King's death. Details of Lilly's judgment were made public – that the King would be sentenced to execution, but should he live to 31 January there was reason to be optimistic about his fate. Accusations surfaced that Lilly used this information to advise the Council of War on a swift trial, and potentially helped elect the date for his execution. If the commissioners sentenced Charles I to die before the thirty-first of that month, they would be successful; if not, they may see their window of opportunity close forever. These allegations would be very dangerous for Lilly after the restoration of monarchy in 1660, when many people were brought to trial and executed for the regicide of the late Stuart king. Lilly responds:

> Against this absurd untruth I absolutely protest, and do deny, that either privately or publicly I advised his death, either to the Soldiery or any other Authority. My own thoughts were ever he would die a violent death, for his Nativity did promise so much; which was the reason I so many times hinted such a thing in many of my books...

Lilly goes on to discuss the many details of Charles I's nativity that promised a violent end, the most ominous being a lunar eclipse in 8° Gemini that occurred on the King's preceding birthday. This eclipse fell opposite his natal Sun, about which Lilly said "nothing is more fatal." Whether Lilly played an active role in electing the date of a king's execution is open for debate, and the evidence may be merely circumstantial. Regardless, this piece of historical record is of interest when assessing the finer details of the execution recorded in Lilly's autobiography and almanacs.[7]

After the King's death the Rump assumed control of the nation, but the Presbyterian influence in Parliament continued to be divisive and oppressive. By 1652 the Parliament had come to be wholly disdained, not least by the New Model Army and its officers who were so frequently mistreated. Lilly writes in his autobiography,

> The Parliament now grows odious unto all good men, the members whereof became insufferable in their pride, covetousness, self-ends, laziness, minding nothing but how to enrich themselves. Much heart-burning now arose betwixt the Presbyterian and Independent, the latter siding with the army, betwixt whose two judgments there was no medium.

In his *Merlinus Anglicus* for 1652/3, Lilly blasted Parliament for their reckless and self-serving approach to governance. He prophesied, in plain language, that unless Parliament corrected its

---

[7] For more information on Lilly's potential astrological involvement in selecting the date for Charles I's execution, see John S. Dawson's article, "A Time to Die: William Lilly and the Execution of Charles I," *The Astrological Journal* (March/April 2007).

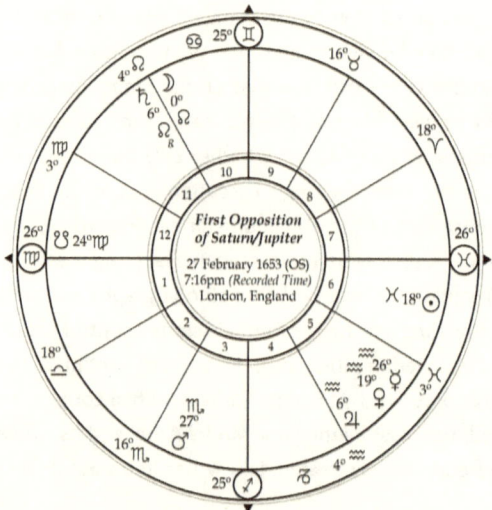

Fig. 5. The Saturn-Jupiter Opposition of 1653

domineering course, the upcoming Saturn/Jupiter opposition of 1653 promised disgrace and a public defeat:

> I pray God make this Parliament wise, the Body of this Fabric standing upon a very tottering Foundation: for if this Authority under which we mourn, after this Opposition of Saturn and Jupiter shall enforce us to some new and illegal Assessment, or by way of raising Money upon any Pretence whatsoever ... I am Confident, we of the Commonalty joining with the Soldier, shall assume so much Liberty to our selves, as to Choose and Elect such Members as hereafter shall be more tender to our Purses, and more Liberal of their own, and we shall endeavour so strictly to call unto account each Member of this Parliament, who hath fingered

our Treasure, that we shall leave many of them as naked as
when they came out of their Mother's wombs, or when first
to be Members of Parliament.

Lilly begins his assessment of this opposition by explaining core mundane principles regarding superior conjunctions and oppositions. As the most superior planet, Saturn has natural signification of those in authority. Leo is described as an overbearing sign, one that makes others desirous of power and rule. Saturn has recently entered Leo where it has no dignity or dominion, which signifies the usurping of authority from its rightful owners. Lilly further demonstrates the unfortunate condition of the people by the South Node's presence on the first house cusp.

Trouble comes for those in power when Saturn meets another superior planet in hard aspect. In early 1563, Jupiter comes to opposition and challenges Saturn's rule. Lilly makes the comment that the people will join together with the soldiers to oust Parliament from their seats. A well-dignified Mars in tight sextile to the ascendant shows support to and from the people of England, while a square to tenth house ruler Mercury promises a forcible overthrow. In mundane figures, the Moon also has a role of showing the country's common people. She is plugging into the Saturn/Jupiter opposition by an applying conjunction to Saturn. Together these significations help us understand why Jupiter, in opposition to Saturn, signifies the people and soldiery uniting to "enforce the election of new members."

As it happens, this connection between people and soldiery is beautifully reinforced by the national chart of England (1066 – Coronation of William). In that chart, Aries rises with Mars in the eleventh house at 8° Aquarius, conjunct Jupiter in the opposition chart. Mars rules the first house and signifies the people of England, but on the level of natural signification also shows the British soldiers.

Perhaps the most overlooked feature of Lilly's judgment lies in the phrase, "the Body of this Fabric standing upon a very tottering foundation." In her own commentary on this chart Deborah Houlding has provided thoughts on the intention behind these words, stating that they appear to come from Jupiter's rulership over the fourth house of foundations, and that we find him in direct opposition to another superior body.[8] Oppositions show sudden breaks, changes, shocks, and upsets.

Lilly's was a loaded prognostication, and one Parliament was not to take lightly. Here he not only warns Parliament about their future decisions, but implies in his phrasing "some new and illegal Assessment," that Parliament had already been acting well outside their legal limitations. Concerned that Lilly's words could stir up a riotous response from the common folk, Lilly was called to stand trial before a Parliamentary committee.

To his great fortune, one member of that committee, Speaker Lenthall, not only notified Lilly that he was due to be summoned, but identified the passages that had acerbated Parliament. Lilly rushed over to his printer and requested six copies of his 1652/3 *Anglicus* to be reprinted. Lilly was careful to either change or delete entirely those passages that riled Parliament, and left the publisher with six new (albeit tampered) copies of the 1652/3 *Anglicus*.

---

8 Deborah Houlding, "An Introduction to Horary Astrology, Part I: Considerations before Study and Cautionary Tales from History," *The Mountain Astrologer* 165 (October, 2012): 40.

At the start of the trial, an original copy of *Anglicus* was produced. Lilly was asked to inspect the volume and confirm that it was his own almanac. After he pretended to scan and inspect the pages, Lilly responded, "This is none of my book, some malicious Presbyterian hath wrote it, who are my mortal enemies; I disown it." He then pulled the six revised copies of his *Anglicus* from his pocket, labeling them as his own.

The committee was stunned and speechless. An outright lie though it was, the hesitation it caused saved Lilly from a guilty verdict and may have spared his life. Committee members spent their time bickering over whether or not Lilly's testimony was honest. If his testimony was false, Parliament would be vindicated though not free of criticism from the common people for censoring their beloved astrologer. If Lilly was telling the truth, Parliament would be responsible for imprisoning an innocent and influential man. Surely, one member argued, Lilly would write about the injustice in his next almanac, and where would Parliament be with the people then? A committee member voiced concern that a misstep by Parliament in handling Lilly's case would be disastrous: "I must tell you, I fear the consequence urged out of the book will prove effectually true. It is my counsel, to admonish him hereafter to be more wary, and for the present to dismiss him." Lilly was sent to prison while the committee attempted to sort through their confusion.

As Lilly was being escorted out of the courtroom, Oliver Cromwell entered and called for him to be brought back in. Cromwell looked Lilly over for a moment then permitted the bailiff to remove him from the room. Cromwell acted on Lilly's behalf to have him acquitted, which was not hard work considering how delicate a situation Lilly's trial turned out to be. The charges were officially dropped thirteen days later, due in large part to Cromwell's pressure, but also to the committee's exasperation and inability to find a justifiable step forward.

The Rump at that time was struggling to keep a hold on its own affairs. Continually plagued by in-fighting and indecisive leadership, the members proved more concerned with their own position of power than the country they were meant to be governing. A man of notoriously short patience, Cromwell decided to take matters into his own hands and, perhaps knowingly, activated Lilly's controversial prophecy. On 20 April 1653 (OS) at 11AM, Cromwell stormed Parliament with a troop of his musketeers, drove the members out of Westminster, and forcibly dissolved the Rump Parliament. Cromwell would eventually take on the role of Protector in what would later be called Cromwell's Protectorate.

In her research, Houlding has speculated that Cromwell's seizure of Parliament was either astrologically elected, or serves to illustrate how astrological cycles come together over time. Cromwell entered Westminster when the Moon had come to conjoin the tenth house cusp of the Saturn/Jupiter opposition chart. Mars had moved to the first degree of Sagittarius, in a partile (exact by degree) trine to the opposition chart's Moon. The Mars/Moon connection wonderfully illustrates, through natural signification, the soldiers enforcing the will of the public. Mercury, the tenth house ruler in the opposition chart, changed signs within hours of Cromwell's victorious overthrow. It is a mundane astrological principle that when the ruler of the tenth house changes signs, there is a change in who holds power. Mercury moved from the fixed, stubborn sign of Taurus to his own domicile Gemini on the afternoon of 20 April (OS), auguring a more agreeable period ahead.

Introduction

Over the coming years Lilly would endure a few more political scuffles and be brought to court again, but he worked very hard to avoid controversy in his later days. At the close of Lilly's life, he was practicing medicine in the countryside, far from the raucous nature of London living. He looked after all manner of clients, including the devastatingly poor who could not afford proper treatment. In one letter to his friend Elias Ashmole, Lilly hilariously writes, "An aged woman, 85, sent me 4d to preserve her to 105. I am persuaded I shall cozen her, but I took her groat, fearing I should get no more that day; but 2s came afterward. You see how I thrive."

In his old age he began to lose his eyesight but was still able to publish annual almanacs through dictation to his adopted son Henry Coley. Richard Saunders, friend and peer of Lilly, went on to write a volume called *The Astrological Judgement and Practice of Physick* for which Lilly penned an eloquent introduction. Lilly died a few years later on 9 June 1681 (OS) in his home in Hersham, leaving this world on the third of three consecutive sneezes.

Over the past three or four decades, Lilly's work has enjoyed a re-emergence into popular focus. In 1975, Derek Parker published a thorough biography on Lilly's life, *Familiar to All*. Throughout the biography Parker retained skeptical, sometimes outright negative attitudes towards Lilly and horary, at one point saying, "Horary astrology is now generally discredited. But Lilly's clients accepted it. They had to; there was, generally speaking, nothing else available to them. And it did not occur to Lilly to doubt the proposition that it was a proper way of going about things."[9] Still, Parker's research remains valuable to modern students wishing to gain a

---

9 Derek Parker, *Familiar to All: William Lilly and Astrology in the Seventeenth Century* (London: Jonathan Cape Ltd., 1975), 127.

deeper appreciation for the context of life and astrology in seventeenth-century England.

Horary was strongly championed in 1970s England by Derek Appleby and Geoffrey Cornelius, among others. Appleby wrote a primer to the subject, *Horary Astrology: An Introduction to the Astrology of Time*, in 1985, republished in 2005 with a foreword by Cornelius, and it remains an excellent read. Appleby's influence in English astrological circles, including his involvement with the Company of Astrologers (founded by Cornelius, then President of the Astrological Lodge of London, and the Lodge's secretary Maggie Hyde), is largely responsible for the revival of horary astrology in the United Kingdom.

In 1980, Olivia Barclay obtained a rare copy of *Christian Astrology*. Barclay soon found that Zadkiel's nineteenth-century version of *Christian Astrology*, the copy that contemporary century astrologers had been referencing, was an adapted version that removed several significant passages and reworded others in such a way that the intended meaning was diluted, misinterpreted, or altogether lost. In partnership with Catriona Mundle and Clive Kavan of Regulus Publishing, a new facsimile was put forward in 1985.

Barclay set up her own course teaching horary astrology, the Qualifying Horary Practitioner's Course (or QHP), based almost entirely on Lilly's presented technique in *Christian Astrology*. Many of her students went on to have promising careers of their own. Carol Wiggers and J. Lee Lehman were students of Barclay, establishing their own schools and publishing on traditional astrology in the United States. In the United Kingdom notable students include Deborah Houlding, founder of the School of Traditional Astrology and creator of *The Traditional Astrologer* magazine, which ran from 1993 to 2000; John Frawley, astrology teacher and publisher of *The Astrologer's Apprentice* magazine from 1996 to 2001; and Sue Ward, who runs her own course on traditional astrology.

The year 1993 saw another important development in the traditional revival – the founding of Project Hindsight, backed by the three Roberts – Hand, Schmidt, and Zoller. From their work, and through Robert Hand's ARHAT, or *Archives* (originally "Association") *for the Retrieval of Historical Astrological Texts,* and new translations being regularly published by Benjamin Dykes, among others, we now have access to countless historical treatises that better inform our understanding of traditional astrology.

But there comes no change without its detractors, and the current traditional revival we are experiencing has created something of a cultural rift in the global astrological community. Accusations are launched on either side, many of them unfair critiques that have more to say about the attacker than they do about the attacked.

In an attempt to distance themselves from modern astrology, traditional astrologers swing the pendulum far enough back to miss the important work being done today in the field of psychological astrology. As a horary astrologer I have seen firsthand how much counseling goes into the consultation process, and that aspect of the job is not emphasized enough in traditional circles today. Skill in counseling must be developed alongside analytical skills used to read, dissect, and interpret texts from ancient periods. The chart itself is a symbol of the native or querent, rich in psychological insight, waiting to be judiciously extracted and explored – and there can be nothing more practically useful than facilitating a client's process of actualizing self-awareness.

Today's traditional astrologers are also unjustly critical of those who practiced horary in the nineteenth and early twentieth centuries. Horary was very much alive in America, even as it fell into disrepute in post-Renaissance Europe. Astrologers such as Charles Hatfield, Ivy Goldstein-Jacobson, Robert DeLuce, Evangeline Adams, C. C. Zain, Marc Edmund Jones, and even Dane Rudhyar (who said horary was "a sign of the conscious binding of the individual to the rhythm and purpose of the universal Whole in which he accepts full and deliberate participation"),[10] did remarkable practical and theoretical work with what few texts and resources they had available. We certainly look at horary differently now than these practitioners did thanks to the research and discoveries that better inform our practice. Still, development and discovery will continue into the future and soon our current understanding may not only seem antiquated, but simple and quaint. I hope future generations of astrologers are far kinder to us than we have been to our own astrological ancestry.

Conversely, where practitioners of psychological astrology tend to err stems from a superficial knowledge of the history and development of astrological symbolism. An excellent and simple example is the modern approach to house meanings. Many modern textbooks take on the view that the houses symbolize, in sequence, the psychological development of a person. As Houlding has pointed out in her *Temples of the Sky*, this pattern seems to hold up for the first few houses, but begins to fall apart when we see that the psychological experience of pregnancy comes before the house of relationships, and the house of death comes before the house of career.[11]

---

10 Dane Rudhyar, *The Practice of Astrology* (Stanwood, WA: Sabian Publishing Society, 1969), 139.
11 Deborah Houlding, *The Houses: Temples of the Sky* (Bournemouth, UK: The Wessex Astrologer Ltd., 2006), xv.

Neither were the houses directly associated with the natural order of the Western tropical zodiac (first house equals Aries, second house equals Taurus, and so on). In fact, the houses were numbered in their order to reflect diurnal movement of the heavenly sphere, each house representing one of the two-hour Egyptian watches. Those planets and stars in the first house were first to rise over the eastern horizon; those planets and stars in the second house, second to rise, etc. It was from this order of ascension, called primary motion, that the houses received their numbering.

Historically, assessment of life stages was approached in exactly the reverse order, following the diurnal motion of the life-giving Sun. The first quadrant (twelfth, eleventh, and tenth houses) marks a person in their youth, just as the Sun ascending over the horizon heralds the beginning of a new day. As the Sun passes over the MC it enters the second quarter of its diurnal cycle, and so the second quadrant (ninth, eighth, and seventh houses) represents young adulthood or the second quarter of life. The Sun descends to the cusp of the seventh and sets on young adulthood, and enters the third quadrant of the horoscope (sixth, fifth, and fourth houses). Thus, the third quadrant came to symbolize middle age. The final quadrant (third, second, and first houses) marks the end of the Sun's diurnal cycle, starting from the depths of the chart at the IC and moving upwards toward its rebirth at sunrise. The fourth quadrant offers signification of old age and the final stages of one's life. Traditional texts tell us that we can speculate which years of life are going to be most enjoyable by the quadrant(s) housing the benefics, and the inverse from those quadrants that hold the malefics.

We also see a tendency to lose symbolic associations with modern equations like *planet equals sign equals house* (e.g., Jupiter = Sagittarius = ninth house). We are now beginning to hear, for the first time in astrological history, that Sagittarius bears signification of long journeys, religion and higher education, philosophy, law and lawyers, and the search for truth, when these more properly belong to other astrological bodies or places. We abandon wholesale rich symbolic associations with Sagittarius by giving it the same interpretive function as its ruler Jupiter, and worse, the ninth house, a false correlate made simply because Sagittarius is the ninth sign in the tropical zodiac.

The symbolism of the ninth house primarily derives from it being in the diurnal hemisphere, in trine aspect to the ascendant, opposite the third house, and the joy (or, as Manilius calls it, the "temple") of the illuminating Sun. Its symbolism does not derive from any affinity with Sagittarius, nor from Jupiter, because planets, signs, and houses have separate roles in astrological judgment. Houses *locate*, planets *signify*, and signs *describe*.

Traditional texts give us a more nuanced appreciation for Sagittarius and its unique qualities. It is eastern (veering south), bicorporal or double-bodied, bestial in its second half, ruling places exposed to fire or heat and lands that are hilly and open. Spain, horses, the colors red and royal blue, hips, thighs and buttocks all fall under its significations. In voyages and flights, it signifies the mariners or passengers themselves. These specific descriptions are tremendously useful in horoscope analysis, and are regrettably forfeited when we equate planets to signs to houses.

To divorce a symbol from its history, whether by new invention or lack of knowledge, dulls the astrological blade and weakens the power of the symbol itself. Wooly abstractions on cosmic patterns result, and the ability to leverage the core message of a sign, planet, or house is lost. Language becomes inarticulate, and anything is made to mean anything. Making useful predictions becomes, as many of today's psychological astrologers attest, "impossible." We know something different from history – not only is it possible, but it is useful, and is the heritage of our art.

There has also been an unfair assumption that traditional astrology makes no room for free will. A brief perusal of Lilly's work shows him to be a humanist astrologer, valuing the moral and active agency of his clients. Lilly was very much focused on how he could assist his querent, or those affected by the outcome of a judgment, in attaining more favorable ends. In "A Lady, if marry the Gentleman desired?" Lilly finds grim prospects and says so outright. After seeing his querent's dismay, he looks further to find a helpful aspect from Jupiter, who signified a mutual friend. Lilly encourages the querent to approach this Jupiterian friend to advocate on her behalf. She does so within the timeframe Lilly specifies, and through this friend's help the querent was able to successfully marry the gentleman who had captured her heart.

In "If attain Philosopher's Stone?" Lilly saw that the querent did not have a mind discerning enough to acquire the ultimate alchemical prize. Lilly uncovered warnings of illness in the horary figure, interpreting beyond the limitations of the question to inform the querent that he should be mindful of his health and take precautionary measures. In so doing, he redirected the querent's focus for the betterment of his life.

One querent approached Lilly with concerns about dreams that were disturbing him throughout the night. Lilly's judgment, "Terrible dreams?", demonstrates how Lilly was able to show that the dreams were a subconscious reflection of the worries that plagued the querent's mind the whole day long. Through the application of astrological symbolism Lilly was able to isolate the causes of the querent's stress, aid him in working through the problem and assure the querent that he was exaggerating the misfortune. This gave the querent much-needed peace of mind.

Even to the extent that he was advising against his own interests in "If the Presbytery shall stand?" Lilly made a firm case that the Presbytery could find more sympathy with the army, gentry and populace if it eased off its burdensome approach to civil governance. The Presbytery failed to take note of the warning published in *Christian Astrology*, and the rest, as they say, is history.

Lilly wasn't an isolated example of a free-will approach to astrology. Thomas Aquinas, thirteenth-century Catholic apologist and theologian, made a very convincing argument why predictions can be made from the stars, and how this does not supplant the existence of free will:

> The majority of men follow their passions, which are movements of the sensitive appetite, in which movements of the heavenly bodies can cooperate: but few are wise enough to resist these passions. Consequently, astrologers are able to foretell the truth in the majority of cases, especially in a general way. But not in particular cases; for nothing prevents man resisting his passions by his free-will. Wherefore the astrologers themselves are wont to say that "the wise man is stronger than the stars," forasmuch as, to wit, he conquers his passions.[12]

---

12 Thomas Aquinas, *The Summa Theologica* (New York: Benziger Bros., 1947), 1a, q 115, a4.

Introduction

Albertus Magnus, thirteenth-century friar and bishop of the Roman Catholic Church, made defense for judicial astrology, particularly interrogational astrology, where the question of free will is frequently raised:

> God knew from eternity which of these [options man] would choose. For which reason, in the book of the universe, which is the vellum of heaven, He was able to configure, if He wished, what He knew; if He did this, then the compatibility of free will with divine providence or with the indication of an interrogation is the same. Therefore, if it cannot be denied that divine providence co-exists with free will, it cannot be denied that the profession of interrogations co-exists with it as well.[13]

Albertus Magnus has more potent things to say in his *Speculum Astronomiae*, but his succinct conclusion above suffices. In the same century, Gerard of Feltre addressed the problem of assuming that the course of the stars shows an unchangeable fate in his *Summa on the Stars*: "If the stars make a man a murderer or a thief, then all the more it is the first cause, God, who does this, which is shameful to suggest."[14]

What these comments show is that the concern over free will is not a new one. It has been discussed and explored throughout the centuries, and compelling cases are made by theologians,

---

13 Albertus Magnus, "Speculum Astronomiae" in *The Speculum Astronomiae and Its Enigma – Astrology, Theology and Science in Albertus Magnus and His Contemporaries*, ed. Robert S. Cohen, (Dordrecht: Kluwer Academic Publishers, 1992), 267.

14 Richard Kieckhefer, *Magic in the Middle Ages* (Cambridge: Cambridge University Press, 2000), 128.

astrologers, and philosophers who argue the non-fatalistic nature of judicial astrology. Astrology was never permitted to take on a fatalistic tone as this would have brought direct condemnation from the Church. Rather, the historical approach saw astrology as a tool to *rectify* God-given free will and moral agency.[15]

Traditional and psychological techniques do not have to function at each other's expense. They can (and ought to) co-exist in their own right. Each is able to offer something unique and of use, so long as the symbolism employed does not abandon its historical root but rather grows out from it. While we are in the grips of restoring lost technique today, there must be a caution not to over-develop our predictive muscles while leaving our counseling muscles atrophied. Engaging the precision and artistry of one with the client-centric mindset of the other produces the best and most adept astrologers whose practice fires on all cylinders.

The tradition is not static, even though some speak of it as if it only exists in the past. It is here in the present, and will extend into the future. Though the contemporary community is divided philosophically, there are early signs of healing. In the seventeenth century, astrologers hosted an annual Feast of Mathematicians, where astrologers came together, laid aside their differences – Wharton next to Booker, Lilly next to Gadbury – to celebrate their shared love of astrology. Today we have astrological conferences that provide a similar opportunity to learn and socialize despite theoretical divides. Held across the world by various people and

---

15 Sue Toohey, "And let them be for signs: Albertus Magnus & Prognostication by the Stars," 2006; http://www.skyscript.co.uk/magnus.html [Accessed 7 March 2015].

organizations, conferences encourage us to focus on the social element of our art, and through co-education, advance the art of astrology itself. We are reminded that whether we label ourselves medieval or modern psychological, classical or evolutionary, we are all *contemporary* astrologers who carry the torch of the astrological tradition forward.

Lilly's text forms a keystone around which we are building our astrological foundation. As I read through it, again and again, I found Lilly's material to be denser and more spiritually profound than anticipated. Certain passages ran through my mind from sun-up to sun-down, and some still do. Though the seed Lilly's work planted has been watered by others, it was Lilly who first illustrated to me that horary is not about mere prediction, but igniting the inner spark of self-awareness, reuniting the querent with their own internal compass – their unique macrocosmic link – in order to assist them as they work through some of their most perplexing and challenging life problems.

When I first picked up William Lilly's autobiography to learn more about his life and times, I found myself flying through the pages with a low retention rate. I knew nothing of the socio-political context of Lilly's day, nor did I have functioning knowledge of seventeenth-century England's government structure. I set out to fully annotate this volume for myself, to understand small points in Lilly's writing that might otherwise seem unremarkable or inconsequential – names, places, event details, etc. Now that it is being made public, my vision for this annotated volume is that it assists others in reading primary source material on Lilly's life. Though secondary sources are informative reads in themselves, nothing supplants the magic of Lilly's own autobiography. With nearly three hundred annotations, this volume should adequately enable students in astrology to engage in Lilly's work without requiring a mound of companion volumes to their left and right (as I had).

Regardless of one's philosophical leanings, it is important for today's astrologer to be familiar with Lilly and his works. He was perhaps the last great astrologer before the break in the astrological lineage that happened after the seventeenth century. Anyone wishing to get a better understanding of our history should read and study Lilly's autobiography, a vivid text that will cultivate appreciation for the difficulties our art has endured.

WADE CAVES
San Francisco, May 2015

Footnotes by the historical editor, ELIAS ASHMOLE (1617–1692), appear in the text with asterisks (*) and daggers (†, ‡) as in the 1822 edition. All numbered footnotes are by WADE CAVES.

ADVERTISEMENT

PREFIXED TO THE LIVES OF ELIAS ASHMOLE & WILLIAM LILLY

IN 1 VOL. 8VO. 1772.

Although we cannot, with justice, compare Elias Ashmole to that excellent Antiquary John Leland, or William Lilly to the learned and indefatigable Thomas Hearne; yet I think we may fairly rank them with such writers as honest Anthony Wood,[1] *whose* Diary *greatly resembles that of his cotemporary, and intimate friend, Elias Ashmole.*

Some anecdotes, connected with affairs of state; many particulars relating to illustrious persons, and antient and noble families; several occurrences in which the Public is interested, and other matters of a more private nature, can only be found in works of this kind. History cannot stoop to the meanness of examining the materials of which Memoirs *are*

---

1 Leland (sometimes Leyland), Hearne and Wood were noted English antiquarians – Leland in the sixteenth century, Wood in the seventeenth, and Hearne in the eighteenth. William Huddesford, the Keeper (i.e., curator) of the Ashmolean Museum from 1755 to 1772, wrote on these three historians in *Lives of Leland, Hearne and Wood* (Oxford, 1772).

generally composed. And yet the pleasure and benefit resulting from such books are manifest to every reader.

I hope the admirers of the very laborious Thomas Hearne will pardon me, if I should venture to give it as my opinion, and with much deference to their judgment, that William Lilly's Life and Death of Charles the first[2] *contains more useful matter of instruction, as well as more splendid and striking occurrences, than are to be found in several of those monkish volumes published by that learned Oxonian.*

Lilly affords us many curious particulars relating to the life of that unfortunate Prince, which are no where else to be found. In delineating the character of Charles, he seems dispassionate and impartial, and indeed it agrees perfectly with the general portraiture of him, as it is drawn by our most authentic historians.[3]

---

2 An integral part of the work *Monarchy or No Monarchy in England* published in 1651, which sought to discover astrologically whether England would continue to be governed by monarchs, and what troubles Parliament might face in the wake of King Charles I's execution.

3 King Charles I was a well-known patron of the arts with a great number of supporters. The King's troubles came from his frequent dissolution of Parliament and attempts to govern without a legislative body to hold his powers in check. Understandably, this did not sit well with the people of England, and his opponents began to paint him as an oppressive tyrant. John Dawson, in his article "A Time To Die: William Lilly and the Execution of Charles I," said this in introduction to the King's reign:

> Charles Stuart of England was a king who firmly believed he ruled by divine right. It was his obsessive need to be an absolute ruler that ultimately led to his downfall. Instead of concentrating on running the country efficiently, he constantly used the common people as a club to gain control over the Church and Parliament. After his defeat and

ADVERTISEMENT

The History of Lilly's Life and Times *is certainly one of the most entertaining narratives in our language. With respect to the science he professed of calculating nativities, casting figures, the prediction of events, and other appendages of astrology, he would fain make us think that he was a very solemn and serious believer. Indeed, such is the manner*

> capture by the army, the King was held prisoner in a number of locations, [...] finally in London where his fate was to be decided. After years of Civil War, the army had had enough and sought to bring the bloodshed to an end. A majority within Parliament (who had a vested interest) were happy to keep Charles as monarch as long as he promised to take into account the people's grievances. But Charles was just not able to embrace the word "compromise" and continued in his old ways of scheming and intrigue. Obstinately, he went back on his promises and began to secretly organise a third civil war by inviting both the Scots and Irish to invade England. This was the final straw; those in Parliament that had managed to live through the slaughter of the last six years were now in no mood for forgiveness and so laid their plans to rid themselves of what they saw as an untrustworthy, tyrannical megalomaniac. They believed (correctly) that whilst ever Charles I lived, there would be no peace in England. (*The Astrological Journal*, Mar/Apr 2007).

Still, the beheading of King Charles I in 1649 truly shocked Lilly and many who clamored for an end to monarchy. After his execution, Lilly writes candidly of Charles I's qualities in *Observations*, saying,

> To speak truly of him, he had many singular parts in nature; he was an excellent horseman, would shoot well at a mark, had singular skill in limning and pictures, a good mathematician, not unskillful in music, well read in divinity, excellently in history, and no less in the laws and statues of this nation; he had a quick and sharp conception, would write his mind singularly well, and in good language and style, only he loved long Parenthesis...

of telling his story, that sometimes the reader may possibly be induced to suppose Lilly rather an enthusiast than an impostor. He relates many anecdotes of the pretenders to foretell events, raise spirits, and other impostures, with such seeming candor, and with such an artless simplicity of style, that we are almost persuaded to take his word when he protests such an inviolable respect to truth and sincerity.

The powerful genius of Shakespeare could carry him triumphantly through subjects the most unpromising, and fables the most improbable: we therefore cannot wonder at the success of such of his plays, where the magic of witches and the incantation of spirits are described, or where the power of fairies is introduced; when such was the credulity of the times respecting these imaginary beings, and when that belief was made a science of, and kept alive by artful and superstitious, knavish, and enthusiastic teachers; what Lilly relates of these people, considered only as matter of fact, is surely very curious.

To conclude; I know no record but this where we can find so just and so entertaining a History of Doctor Dee, Doctor Forman, Booker, Winder, Kelly, Evans, (Lilly's Master,) the famous William Poole, and Captain Bubb Fiske, Sarah Shelborne, and many others.

To these we may add, the uncommon effects of the Crystal, the appearance of Queen Mabb,[4] and other strange and miraculous operations, which owe their origin to folly, curiosity, superstition, bigotry, and imposture.

---

4 Queen of the Faeries.

WILLIAM LILLY

*From an Original Picture in the
Ashmolean Museum, Oxford*

THE

LIFE

OF

WILLIAM LILLY

STUDENT IN ASTROLOGY

Wrote by himself in the 66th Year of his Age, at Hersham, in the Parish of Walton-upon-Thames, in the County of Surry.   *Propria Manu.*

---

* I WAS BORN in the county of Leicester, in an obscure town, in the north-west borders thereof, called Diseworth,⁵ seven miles south of the town of Derby, one mile from Castle-Donnington, a town of great rudeness, wherein it is not remembered that any of

> * "William Lilly was a prominent, and, in the opinion of many of his cotemporaries, a very important personage

---

5 Diseworth is a small village town in the heart of England, approximately 115 miles northwest of London. As of 2015, residents in this town number in the hundreds.

the farmers thereof did ever educate any of their sons to learning, only my grandfather sent his younger son to Cambridge, whose name was Robert Lilly, and died Vicar of Cambden in Gloucestershire, about 1640.

> in the most eventful period of English history. He was a principal actor in the farcical scenes which diversified the bloody tragedy of civil war; and while the King and the Parliament were striving for mastery in the field, he was deciding their destinies in the closet. The weak and the credulous of both parties, who sought to be instructed in 'destiny's dark counsels,' flocked to consult the 'wily Archimage', who, with exemplary impartiality, meted out victory and good fortune to his clients, according to the extent of their faith, and the weight of their purses. A few profane Cavaliers might make his name the burthen of their *malignant* rhymes – a few of the more scrupulous among the *Saints* might keep aloof in sanctified abhorrence of the 'Stygian sophister'[6] – but the great majority of the people lent a willing and reverential ear to his prophecies and prognostications. Nothing was too high or too low – too mighty or too

---

6 A title that means something akin to "dark philosopher," which (together with the earlier reference to Lilly as "wily Archimage") seems to reflect the author's belief that Lilly's work was more diabolical than it was innocuous. *Stygian* means "of or related to the Styx," the fateful river in Greek mythology that separated the earth from the Underworld. *Sophister* comes from the Greek *sophistês*, meaning "expert," or "wiseman," whose root *sophos* gives us such modern terms as philosophy, theosophy, etc.

The town of Diseworth did formerly belong long unto the Lord Seagrave, for there is one record in the hands of my cousin Melborn Williamson, which mentions one acre of land abutting north upon the gates of the Lord

> insignificant, for the grasp of his genius. The stars, his informants, were as communicative on the most trivial as on the most important subjects. If a scheme was set on foot to rescue the king, or to retrieve a stray trinket – to restore the royal authority, or to make a frail damsel an honest woman – to cure the nation of anarchy, or a lap-dog of a surfeit, William Lilly was the oracle to be consulted. His *almanacks* were spelled over in the tavern and quoted in the senate; they nerved the arm of the soldier, and rounded the periods of the orator. The fashionable beauty, dashing along in her calash from St. James's or the Mall, and the prim, starched dame, from Watling-street or Bucklersbury, with a staid foot-boy, in a plush jerkin, plodding behind her – the reigning toast among 'the men of wit about town', and the leading groaner in a tabernacle concert – glided alternately into the study of the trusty wizard, and poured into his attentive ear strange tales of love, or trade, or treason. The Roundhead stalked in at one door, whilst the Cavalier was hurried out at the other.[7]

---

[7] Lilly lived and practiced astrology during the height of the English Civil War, when the Roundheads (supporters of the Parliament) sought to overcome the Cavaliers (supporters of King Charles I and the monarchy). For much of his life, Lilly was more sympathetic to the Parliamentary cause, and many of his almanacs reflect his heavy criticism of the monarchy. His

Seagrave; and there is one close, called Hall-close, wherein the ruins of some ancient buildings appear, and particularly where the dove-house stood; and there is also the ruins of decayed fish-ponds and other

> "The *Confessions* of a man so variously consulted and trusted, if written with the candour of a Cardan or a Rousseau, would indeed be invaluable. *The Memoirs of William Lilly*, though deficient in this essential ingredient, yet contain a variety of curious and interesting anecdotes of himself and his cotemporaries, which, where the vanity of the writer, or the truth of his art, is not concerned, may be received with implicit credence.
>
> "The simplicity and apparent candour of his narrative might induce a hasty reader of this book to believe him a well-meaning but somewhat silly personage, the dupe of his own speculations – the deceiver of himself as well as of others. But an attentive examination of the events of his life, even as recorded by himself,

outspoken stance did not dissuade members high and low of each faction (and others besides) from consulting him on a wide array of personal and political matters. Lilly made an honest attempt to assist anyone who came for astrological guidance, regardless of their political affiliation, even to the extent that he attempted to help the disgraced Charles I escape imprisonment on three separate occasions.

Not surprisingly, it was fairly common for contemporaries and later commentators to attempt to discredit Lilly for his seemingly opportunistic behavior, but as Derek Parker notes in *Familiar to All*, "if one disengages aftersight, and thinks of Lilly (and thousands like him) trying to resolve his attitudes to a complex political and social situation, it becomes more difficult to condemn him" (London, 1975; 82).

outhouses. This town came at length to be the inheritance of Margaret, Countess of Richmond, mother of Henry VII. which Margaret gave this town and lordship of Diseworth unto Christ's College in Cambridge,

will not warrant so favourable an interpretation. His systematic and successful attention to his own interest – his dexterity in keeping on 'the windy side of the law' – his perfect political pliability – and his presence of mind and fertility of resources when entangled in difficulties – indicate an accomplished impostor, not a crazy enthusiast. It is very possible and probable, that, at the outset of his career, he was a real believer in the truth and lawfulness of his art, and that he afterwards felt no inclination to part with so pleasant and so profitable a delusion: like his patron, Cromwell,[8] whose

---

8 Oliver Cromwell, an English military leader with strong Parliamentary leanings. Cromwell was nicknamed "Ironsides" for his ruthlessness in the pursuit of power, and maintained something of a contentious reputation. He was third to sign the king's death warrant in 1649; and after King Charles I's beheading, Cromwell helped to establish the Commonwealth of England. Thus began the Interregnum, the period between the beheading of Charles I and the restoration of the monarchy in 1660 when Charles II was crowned King.

Cromwell's dissatisfaction with Parliament's infighting and ineffective governance in the Interregnum incited Cromwell to storm Parliament with a band of musketeers, forcibly dismissing the waffling members from their posts. (Lilly predicted this takeover in his 1652/3 *Anglicus*, and would stand trial for the use of his pen against the Rump). Cromwell assumed the role of Lord Protector in 1653, and served in that role until his death by illness in 1658. Despite his vocalized desire to re-instate a period of peace

the Master and Fellows whereof have ever since, and at present, enjoy and possess it.

In the church of this town there is but one monument, and that is a white marble stone, now almost broken

> early fanaticism subsided into hypocrisy, he carefully retained his folly as a cloak for his knavery. Of his success in deception, the present narrative exhibits abundant proofs. The number of his dupes was not confined to the vulgar and illiterate, but included individuals of real worth and learning, of hostile parties and sects, who courted his acquaintance and respected his predictions. His proceedings were deemed of sufficient importance to be twice made the subject of a parliamentary inquiry; and even after the Restoration – when a little more scepticism, if not more wisdom, might have been expected – we find him examined by a Committee of the House of Commons, respecting his fore-knowledge of the great fire of London. We know not whether it 'should more move our anger or our mirth', to see an assemblage of British Senators – the cotemporaries of Hampden and Falkland – of Milton and Clarendon

and harmony in the country, some saw his actions as hypocrisy and little more than an ambitious grab at power, echoed here in this footnote to Lilly's autobiography. After Cromwell's death, the protectorship passed to his son, Richard, but he lacked the gravity and influence of his father and the Protectorate ended in 1659. The monarchy was restored in England in 1660, and soon thereafter Cromwell's decaying body was (reportedly) exhumed and executed posthumously on the twelfth anniversary of Charles I's execution.

to pieces, which was placed there by Robert Lilly, my grandfather, in memory of Jane his wife, the daughter of Mr. Poole of Dalby, in the same county, a family now quite extinguished. My grandmother's brother was Mr.

– in an age which roused into action so many and such mighty energies – gravely engaged in ascertaining the causes of a great national calamity, from the prescience of a knavish fortuneteller, and puzzling their wisdoms to interpret the symbolical flames, which blazed in the mis-shapen wood-cuts of his oracular publications.[9] "As a set-off against these honours may be mentioned, the virulent and unceasing attacks of almost all the party scribblers of the day; but their abuse he shared in common with men, whose talents and virtues have outlived the malice of their cotemporaries, and

'Whose honours with increase of ages grow,
As streams roll down, enlarging as they flow'."
Retrospective Review, Vol. ii. p. 51.[10]

---

9 Lilly included in his *Monarchy or No Monarchy* nineteen hieroglyphics, which, Lilly wrote, "in Ænigmaticall Types, Formes, Figures, Shapes, doth perfectly represent the future condition of the English Nation and Commonwealth for many hundreds of years yet to come." One of these woodcuts is said to have predicted the outbreak of the plague in 1665, and another the Great Fire of London in 1666.

10 The *Retrospective Review* was an antiquary publication that focused on critiques of early books and manuscripts. The articles contained within the *Review* are not credited, though we know it was published by Charles and Henry Baldwin (alternatively spelled Baldwyn in some volumes) in London from 1820 to 1828.

Henry Poole, one of the Knights of Rhodes, or Templars, who being a soldier at Rhodes at the taking thereof by Solyman the Magnificent,[11] and escaping with his life, came afterwards to England, and married the Lady Parron or Perham, of Oxfordshire, and was called, during his life, Sir Henry Poole. William Poole the Astrologer knew him very well, and remembers him to have been a very tall person, and reputed of great strength in his younger years.

The impropriation of this town of Diseworth was formerly the inheritance of three sisters, whereof two became votaries;[12] one in the nunnery of Langly in the parish of Diseworth, valued at the suppression, I mean the whole nunnery, at thirty-two pounds per annum, and this sister's part is yet enjoyed by the family of the Grayes, who now, and for some years past, have the enjoyment and possession of all the lands formerly belonging to the nunnery in the parish of Diseworth, and are at present of the yearly value of three hundred and fifty pounds per annum. One of the sisters gave her part of the great tithes unto a religious house in Bredon upon the Hill; and, as the inhabitants report, became a religious person afterwards.

The third sister married, and her part of the tithes in succeeding ages became the Earl of Huntingdon's, who not many years since sold it to one of his servants.

---

11 Suleiman the Magnificent, Sultan of the Ottoman Empire. In 1522 Suleiman conquered the Christian stronghold of Rhodes that had previously been occupied by the Knights Hospitaller.
12 Nuns.

The donation of the vicarage is in the gift of the Grayes of Langley, unto whom they pay yearly, (I mean unto the Vicar) as I am informed, six pounds per annum. Very lately some charitable citizens have purchased one-third portion of the tithes, and given it for a maintenance of a preaching minister, and it is now of the value of about fifty pounds per annum.

There have been two hermitages in this parish; the last hermit was well remembered by one Thomas Cooke, a very ancient inhabitant, who in my younger years acquainted me therewith.

This town of Diseworth is divided into three parishes; one part belongs under Locington,[13] in which part standeth my father's house, over-against the west end of the steeple, in which I was born: some other farms are in the parish of Bredon, the rest in the parish of Diseworth.

In this town, but in the parish of Lockington, was I born, the first day of May 1602.[14]

---

13 Alternatively, Lockington.

14 Interestingly, Lilly records his birth as 1 May 1602, and in his annual *Anglicus* (almanac) titled *Peace or No Peace* (1645) he states that he was born with Venus cazimi and a Pisces Moon. These chart features are incongruous with a 1 May birth, as that date would give a Capricorn Moon and Venus just outside generally accepted cazimi limits of 17' of arc (though some historical authors did define cazimi as within 1° of the Sun). It is likely that Lilly, the son of a yeoman farmer, was himself unsure of the exact details of his birth data, which can account for variations in recorded information. A birth date for the fifth or sixth of May would offer a Pisces Moon and Venus within 1° of the Sun, but it seems unlikely that Lilly (or his parents) should misremember a birth on 1 May, as this day was celebrated as a public holiday (May Day) with extravagant festitivites.

My father's name was William Lilly, son of Robert, the son of Robert, the son of Rowland, &c. My mother was Alice, the daughter of Edward Barham, of Fiskerton Mills, in Nottinghamshire, two miles from Newark upon Trent: this Edward Barham was born in Norwich,

Lilly's younger contemporary and detractor, John Gadbury, publicly contested Lilly's comments about having a Pisces Moon, instead favoring a date and time rectified by James Blackwell. On page 188 in his *Collection of Nativities* (1662), Gadbury published the following in reference to that rectified figure:

> The person whose geniture this is (to puzzle the understandings of the inquisitous) hath pretended himself to have two several nativities: (1.) In his Almanac of 1645 he tells his reader (in the Epistle thereunto) that he had the Moon in Pisces, which makes him a piece of a good fellow, &c., which (if true) he must be born the 5th or 6th of May 1602. (2.) In his Introduction under his effigies, he says he was born on May 1st 1602, and then the Moon will not be in Pisces but in Capricorn, as in this figure. I am of the opinion he hath not the Moon in Pisces but in Capricorn, and therefore believe this to be his right nativity; the rather because my loving friend Mr. James Blackwell hath proved it so to be by thirteen several arguments or accidents printed a year-and-a-half since by itself. In which little tract, the ingenious Artist may meet with a concise method for calculating and judging a nativity; and unto which I refer the desirous reader for further satisfaction in this geniture. The reason why I am no larger herein is: because I would not be esteemed either envious or partial.

NB: All dates in Lilly's autobiography are recorded in Old Style (OS). Old Style dating adheres to the Julian calendar, replaced in England with the Gregorian calendrical system in 1752 under the Calendar Act of 1750. Converting to New Style (NS) for sixteenth- and seventeenth-century dates requires a correction of +10 days. While Lilly's record would read 1 May 1602 for his birth, we would take that date to be 11 May 1602 in our modern calendrical system.

and well remembered the rebellion of Kett the Tanner, in the days of Edward VI.

Our family have continued many ages in this town as yeomen; besides the farm my father and his ancestors lived in, both my father and grandfather had much free land, and many houses in the town, not belonging to the college, as the farm wherein they were all born doth, and is now at this present of the value of forty pounds per annum, and in possession of my brother's son; but the freehold land and houses, formerly purchased by my ancestors, were all sold by my grandfather and father; so that now our family depend wholly upon a college lease.[15] Of my infancy I can speak little, only I do remember that in the fourth year of my age I had the measles.

I was, during my minority, put to learn at such schools, and of such masters, as the rudeness of the place and country afforded; my mother intending I should be a scholar from my infancy, seeing my father's back-slidings in the world, and no hopes by plain husbandry to recruit a decayed estate; therefore upon Trinity Tues-

---

15 Lilly was born at a time when farmland was experiencing rising valuation and yeoman farmers were beginning to have some degree of financial security. It is notable that Lilly's family owned the land they worked on. This was rare, even amongst the more successful yeoman. Over the years Lilly's father struggled with maintaining the property and slid into substantial debt, eventually landing himself at Leicester Gaol (a variant of "jail") by 1620. Despite the farm's difficulties, Lilly comments that his nephew eventually restored it to much of its former glory, and at the time of Lilly's writing was enjoying the farm's then considerable dividends of £40 per annum.

day,¹⁶ 1613, my father had me to Ashby de la Zouch, to be instructed by one Mr. John Brinsley; one, in those times, of great abilities for instruction of youth in the Latin and Greek tongues; he was very severe in his life and conversation, and did breed up many scholars for the universities: in religion he was a strict Puritan, not conformable wholly to the ceremonies of the Church of England. In this town of Ashby de la Zouch, for many years together, Mr. Arthur Hildersham¹⁷ exercised his ministry at my being there; and all the while I continued at Ashby, he was silenced. This is that famous Hildersham, who left behind him a commentary on the fifty-first psalm; as also many sermons upon the fourth of John, both which are printed; he was an excellent textuary, of exemplary life, pleasant in discourse, a strong enemy to the Brownists,¹⁸ and dissented not from the Church of

England in any article of faith, but only about wearing the surplice, baptizing with the cross, and kneeling at the sacrament; most of the people in town were di-

---

16 Also known as Whit Tuesday and Pentecost Tuesday; the third day of the week that starts with Pentecost. In the Christian tradition, Pentecost was observed seven weeks after Easter Sunday (i.e., the fiftieth day after Easter).

17 The puritan Vicar of Ashby, who renounced the Roman Catholic priesthood for Protestantism. Hildersham and Brinsley shared Puritan ideals, and both endured their fair share of prejudice as a result. Hildersham would later be sent to Fleet Prison, and Brinsley would be removed from his post (for unknown reasons, but we may speculate that the reasons were primarily political).

18 Early separatists from the Church of England, named after Robert Browne.

rected by his judgement, and so continued, and yet do continue presbyterianly affected; for when the Lord of Loughborough in 1642, 1643, 1644, and 1645, had his garrison in that town, if by chance at any time any troops of horse had lodged within the town, though they came late at night to their quarters; yet would one or other of the town presently give Sir John Gell of Derby notice, so that ere next morning most of his Majesty's troops were seized in their lodgings, which moved the Lord of Loughborough merrily to say, there was not a fart let in Ashby, but it was presently carried to Derby.[19]

The several authors I there learned were these, viz. *Sententiæ Pueriles*, *Cato*, *Corderius*, *Æsop's Fables*, *Tully's Offices*, *Ovid de Tristibus*; lastly, *Virgil*, then *Horace*; as

---

19 To those unfamiliar with England's Civil War in the seventeenth century, it may seem strange that Ashby's Presbyterian affections are demonstrated by the reporting of Royalist activity to Sir John Gell (a Roundhead military leader in nearby Derby), and that troops garrisoned in Ashby were swiftly "seized in their lodgings."

The English monarchy had a close relationship with the Church of England, a modestly reformed version of Roman Catholicism that was only begrudgingly tolerant of non-conformity within the Church. To question the Church of England was not just a religious move, but also a political one that some saw as a direct challenge to the monarchy itself. As can be imagined, this put a great deal of social and political pressure on those who subscribed to alternative religious thought, and the champions of religious tolerance (Puritans and Presbyterians among them) tended to favor Parliamentary rule. It was amusing to the Lord of nearby Loughborough, and no doubt to Lilly also, that there was not a whisper of Royalist activity in Ashby that was not immediately reported by the Presbyterians in that town to the Roundhead leaders in Derby for a quick rounding-up of His Majesty's forces.

also *Camden's Greek Grammar*, *Theognis* and *Homer's Iliads*: I was only entered into *Udall's Hebrew Grammar*; he never taught logick, but often would say it was fit to be learned in the universities.

In the fourteenth year of my age, by a fellow scholar of swarth, black complexion, I had like to have my right eye beaten out as we were at play;[20] the same year, about Michaelmas,[21] I got a surfeit,[22] and thereupon a fever, by eating beech-nuts.

In the sixteenth year of my age I was exceedingly troubled in my dreams concerning my salvation and damnation, and also concerning the safety and destruction of the souls of my father and mother; in the nights I frequently wept, prayed and mourned, for fear my sins might offend God.

In the seventeenth year of my age my mother died.

In the eighteenth year of my age my master Brinsley was enforced from keeping school, being persecuted by

---

20 It is an ancient aphorism that afflictions to the luminaries in one's nativity show damage to the eyes. In males, the Sun rules the right eye, the Moon the left. In Lilly's nativity, he has a Sun/Saturn opposition, indicating damage of the nature of Saturn to his right eye ("black eye"). Interestingly, Lilly writes that his attacker was "a scholar of swarth, black complexion," apt descriptions of someone signified by cold and dry Saturn. Lilly later lost his eyesight in his old age, which can be seen by the dual oppositions of the Sun and Saturn, and the Moon and Mars (presuming one uses a birth chart for Lilly with a Pisces Moon).

21 A festival marked in the western Christian tradition to celebrate the archangel Michael, commemorated on 29 September (NS).

22 An excessive amount of something, commonly overeating or overdrinking.

the Bishop's officers; he came to London, and then lectured in London, where he afterwards died. In this year, by reason of my father's poverty, I was also enforced to leave school, and so came to my father's house, where I lived in much penury for one year, and taught school one quarter of a year, until God's providence provided better for me.

For the two laſt years of my being at school, I was of the higheſt form in the school, and chiefeſt of that form; I could then speak Latin as well as English; could make extempore verses upon any theme; all kinds of verses, hexameter, pentameter, phaleuciacks, iambicks, sapphicks, &c. so that if any scholars from remote schools came to dispute, I was ringleader to dispute with them; I could cap verses, &c. If any miniſter came to examine us, I was brought forth againſt him, nor would I argue with him unless in the Latin tongue, which I found few of them could well speak without breaking Priscian's head;[23] which, if once they did, I would complain to my maſter, *Non bene intelligit linguam Latinam, nec prorsus loquitur.*[24] In the derivation of words, I found moſt of them defeċtive, nor indeed were any of them

---

23 To break the rules of prescriptive grammar. Priscianus Caesariensis was a fifth-century Latin grammarian whose master work, *Institutiones Grammaticæ* ("Grammatical Foundations"), formed the curriculum for Latin language education in the medieval period. One would "break Priscian's head" when one violated the fundamental precepts of prescriptive Latin grammar.

24 Roughly, "He does not rightly understand the Latin language, nor does he speak exactly."

good grammarians: all and every of those scholars who were of my form and standing, went to Cambridge and proved excellent divines, only poor I, William Lilly, was not so happy; fortune then frowning upon father's present condition, he not in any capacity to maintain me at the university.[25]

OF THE MANNER HOW I CAME UNTO LONDON

Worthy sir, I take much delight to recount unto you, even all and every circumstance of my life, whether good, moderate, or evil; *Deo gloria*.[26]

My father had one Samuel Smatty for his Attorney, unto whom I went sundry times with letters, who perceiving I was a scholar, and that I lived miserably in the country, losing my time, nor any ways likely to do better, if I continued there; pitying my condition, he sent word for me to come and speak with him, and told me that he had lately been at London, where there was a gentleman wanted a youth, to attend him and his wife, who could write, &c.[27]

---

25 While Lilly lamented that his classmates (to him, the lesser educated) successfully applied themselves to collegiate study while he could not, this would turn out to be of great benefit to Lilly. It allowed him the freedom to move to London, acquire a modest fortune, and eventually learn the art of astrology for which he became internationally famous.

26 "Glory unto God."

27 In the fifteenth and sixteenth centuries, the middle class of London

I acquainted my father with it, who was very willing to be rid of me, for I could not work, drive the plough, or endure any country labour; my father oft would say, I was good for nothing.[28]

I had only twenty shillings, and no more, to buy me a new suit, hose, doublet, &c. my doublet was fustian:[29] I repaired to Mr. Smatty, when I was accoutred, for a letter to my master, which he gave me.

Upon Monday, April 3, 1620, I departed from Diseworth, and came to Leicester: but I must acquaint you, that before I came away I visited my friends, amongst whom I had given me about ten shillings, which was a great comfort unto me. On Tuesday, April the 4th, I took leave of my father, then in Leicester gaol for debt, and came along with Bradshaw the carrier, the same person with whom many of the Duke of Buckingham's kindred had come up with. Hark how the waggons crack with their rich lading! It was a very stormy week, cold and uncomfortable: I footed it all along; we could not reach London until Palm-Sunday, the 9th of April, about half

---

would grow to become a substantial sector of the populace. Despite their growth and fortunate condition, it was not uncommon to find illiterate masters who had need of servants with skill in reading and proper writing.
28 Lilly's father was undergoing trials of his own at this time, dealing with the financial collapse of his farm. It is no surprise that he felt his son, who preferenced language and learning over maintenance of the family farm, was "good for nothing." William Sr. had sold many stakes in his land to repay his debts, but his debts overcame him in the end and he was imprisoned.
29 A thick and durable twill cloth made of flax and cotton, often rough and dyed in dark colors.

an hour after three in the afternoon, at which time we entered Smithfield. When I had gratified the carrier and his servants, I had seven shillings and sixpence left, and no more; one suit of cloaths upon my back, two shirts, three bands, one pair of shoes, and as many stockings. Upon the delivery of my letter my master entertained me, and next day bought me a new cloak, of which you may imagine (good Esquire) whether I was not proud of; besides, I saw and eat good white bread, contrary to our diet in Leicestershire.[30] My master's name was Gilbert Wright, born at Market Bosworth in Leicestershire; my mistress was born at Ashby de la Zouch, in the same county, and in the town where I had gone to school. This Gilbert Wright could neither write nor read: he lived upon his annual rents, was of no calling or profession; he had for many years been servant to the Lady Pawlet in Hertfordshire; and when Serjeant Puckering was made Lord keeper, he made him keeper of his lodgings at Whitehall.[31] When Sir Thomas Egerton was made

---

30 Lilly's father's financial troubles showed in the sorry state of the family meals. Parker notes in his *Familiar to All*, "So young William Lilly grew up in the atmosphere of tightening of belts – to the extent, even, that his mother had to cut down on food, and the wheaten loaf vanished from their table..." (25).

31 Properly the name of a road in Westminster, Whitehall became the moniker of the English governmental administration (much as "Wall Street" is used to refer to the US financial institutions regardless of their actual location). The name "Whitehall" came from The Palace of Whitehall, the primary residence of the English monarchs since the sixteenth century until it was destroyed by a fire in 1698, some eighteen years after Lilly's death. Wright would have looked after the lodgings and accommo-

Lord Chancellor, he entertained him in the same place; and when he married a widow in Newgate Market, the Lord Chancellor recommended him to the company of Salters, London, to admit him into their company, and so they did, and my master in 1624, was master of that company;[32] he was a man of excellent natural parts, and would speak publickly upon any occasion very rationally and to the purpose. I write this, that the world may know he was no taylor, or myself of that or any other calling or profession: my work was to go before my master to church; to attend my master when he went abroad; to make clean his shoes; sweep the street; help to drive bucks when he washed; fetch water in a tub from the Thames: I have helped to carry eighteen tubs of water in one morning; weed the garden; all manner of drudgeries I willingly performed; scrape trenchers, &c. If I had any profession, it was of this nature: I should never have denied being a taylor, had I been one; for there is no calling so base, which by God's mercy may not afford a livelihood; and had not my master entertained me, I would have been of a very mean profession ere I would have returned into the country again; so here ends the actions of eighteen years of my life.

dation of those government officials staying at Whitehall.

32 The joining of such companies was a crucial step in the elevation of one's social standing. Though chartered as a professional guild, these companies served as a symbol of status and social connection. With membership in a well-respected company, one had a substantial platform for municipal office. This was likely Wright's primary interest as he was not a salter by trade.

My master married his second wife for her estate; she was competently rich; she married him for considerations he performed not, (nocturnal society) so that they lived very uncomfortably; she was about seventy years of age, he sixty-six or more; yet never was any woman more jealous of a husband than she; insomuch, that whensoever he went into London, she was confident of his going to women;[33] by those means my life was the more uncomfortable, it being very difficult to please two such opposite natures: however, as to the things of this world I had enough, and endured their discontents with much sereneness. My mistress was very curious to know of such as were then called cunning or wise men, whether she should bury her husband?[34] She frequently visited such persons, and this occasion begot in me a little desire to learn something that way, but wanting money to buy books, I laid aside these motions, and endeavoured to please both master and mistress.

---

33 Humorous gems like these demonstrate Lilly's quick, dry wit (his nativity features a close trine between Mercury in Taurus and Mars in Virgo), and it is easy to imagine a sly smile creeping across his face as he makes this note. One wonders, in light of her advanced age, if Wright making good on these "considerations he performed not" could have curtailed his wife's jealousy.

34 I.e., whether Wright or his wife would die first.

OF MY MISTRESS'S DEATH, AND OCCASION THEREOF BY MEANS OF A CANCER IN HER BREAST

In 1622 she complained of a pain in her left breaſt, whereon there appeared at firſt a hard knob no bigger than a small pea; it increased in a little time very much, was very hard, and sometimes would look very red; she took advice of surgeons, had oils, sear-cloths,[35] plates of lead, and what not: in 1623 it grew very big, and spread all over her breaſt; then for many weeks poultices were applied to it, which in continuance of time broke the skin, and then abundance of watery thin ſtuff came from it, but nothing else; at length the matter came to suppuration,[36] but never any great ſtore issued forth; it was exceeding noisome and painful; from the beginning of it until she died, she would permit no surgeon to dress it but only myself; I applied every thing unto it, and her pains were so great the winter before she died, that I have been called out of my bed two or three times in one night to dress it and change plaiſters. In 1624 by degrees, with scissars, I cut all the whole breaſt away, I mean the sinews, nerves, &c.[37] In one fortnight, or little more, it

---

35 Alternatively, cerecloth – a cloth that is covered in wax, typically used to cover the dead.

36 The discharging of pus.

37 Though saddening, this was undoubtedly a fascinating procedure to young Lilly, who would spend the final years of his life removed to the country, studying and practicing medicine (or "physick") upon any who came to him, including the devastatingly poor without means to pay.

appeared, as it were, mere flesh, all raw, so that she could scarce endure any unguent to be applied.

I remember there was a great cleft through the middle of the breast, which when that fully appeared she died, which was in September 1624; my master being then in the country, his kindred in London would willingly have had mourning for her; but by advice of an especial friend of his I contradicted them; nor would I permit them to look into any chest or trunk in the house. She was decently buried, and so fond of me in the time of her sickness, she would never permit me out of her chamber, gave me five pounds in old gold, and sent me unto a private trunk of her's at a friend's house, where she had one hundred pounds in gold; she bid me bring it away and take it, but when I opened the trunk I found nothing therein; for a kinsman of hers had been there a few days before, and carried all away: she was in a great passion at my relating thereof, because she could not gratify my pains in all her sickness, advised me to help myself, when she was gone, out of my master's goods, which I never did.[38]

Courteous Esquire, be not weary of reading hereof, or what followeth.

When my mistress died, she had under her arm-hole a small scarlet bag full of many things, which, one that

---

38 That Lilly's mistress would suggest this as payment for Lilly's attention and care is indicative of the difficult nature of her marriage to Mr. Wright. It has been noted by many later commentators that it was wise of Lilly to refuse this offer, for many of his later blessings regarding Mr. Wright's estate would never have come to pass.

was there delivered unto me. There was in this bag several sigils,[39] some of Jupiter in Trine, others of the nature of Venus, some of iron, and one of gold, of pure angel-gold,[40] of the bigness of a thirty-three shilling piece of King James's coin. In the circumference on one side was engraven, *Vicit Leo de tribu Judæ Tetragrammaton* +,[41] within the middle there was engraven a holy lamb.[42] In the other circumference there was Amraphel[43] and three +.

---

39 Talismans, said to embody various magical or sacred properties that are conveyed onto their possessors, each according to its design (e.g., for healing, for protection, etc.).

40 A purer gold of higher value than crown or foreign gold, traditionally given to those with a disease known as "king's evil" (today called scrofula, a form of tuberculosis affecting the lymph nodes of the neck). It was believed these coins had the power to heal by way of "royal touch."

41 "The Lion of the Tribe of Judah is victorious." This phrase reflects the passage in Revelation 5:5 (King James' Version) — "And one of the elders saith unto me, Weep not: behold, the Lion of the tribe of Judah, the Root of David, hath prevailed to open the book, and to loose the seven seals thereof." The Lion of Judah is widely believed by Christians to be a symbol of Jesus Christ. The Tetragrammaton (meaning "four letters") was the name for the theonym יהוה thought to hold potent spiritual power as one of the names of the Judeo-Christian god. The Tetragrammaton derived from a Hebrew verb meaning "to be" or "to exist," from which we get the transliterated YHWH (Yahweh) or JHVH (Jehovah).

42 The lamb is a Christian symbol of Christ's corporal sacrifice for the sins of the world.

43 An ancient king of Shinar (Sumer, or Babylonia), briefly written of in the Old Testament Book of Genesis. Amraphel, in conjunction with three other Mesopotamian kings, defeated the five kingdoms of the Jordan plains (Admah, Bela, Gomorrah, Sodom, and Zeboyim) in the biblical War of the Nine Kings (Genesis 14: 1–12). Amongst Amraphel's captives was Abram's son, Lot, who would later be a central character in the tale of So-

In the middle, *Sanctus Petrus*,⁴⁴ *Alpha* and *Omega*.⁴⁵

The occasion of framing this sigil was thus; her former husband travelling into Sussex, happened to lodge in an inn, and to lie in a chamber thereof; wherein, not many months before, a country grazier⁴⁶ had lain, and in the night cut his own throat; after this night's lodging, he was perpetually, and for many years, followed by a spirit, which vocally and articulately provoked him to cut his throat: he was used frequently to say, 'I defy thee, I defy thee', and to spit at the spirit; this spirit followed him many years, he not making any body acquainted with it; at laſt he grew melancholy and discontented; which being carefully observed by his wife, she many times hearing him pronounce, 'I defy thee', &c. she desired him to acquaint her with the cause of his diſtemper, which he then did. Away she went to Dr. Simon Forman, who lived then in Lambeth,⁴⁷ and acquaints him with it; who having framed this sigil, and hanged it about his neck, he wearing it continually until he died, was never more moleſted by the spirit: I sold the sigil for

---

dom and Gomorrah's fall. Scholars have since speculated that Amraphel may have been an alternate name for Hammurabi, the famed Babylonian king whose laws became known as *Hammurabi's Code*.

44 "Saint Peter." In Matthew 16:18, Christ said in reference to Peter, "upon this rock I will build my church." *Petra* means "rock" in Latin.

45 A title attributed by early Christians to both God and Christ, found in Revelation 21:6 and 22:13. *Alpha* and *omega* are the first and last letters of the Greek alphabet, symbolically used to represent the omnipotence and omnipresence of the Christian godhead – "the beginning and the end."

46 Someone who rears and fattens sheep and cattle for market.

47 A district in central London.

DR. SIMON FORMAN

From a Scarce Print

thirty-two shillings, but transcribed the words *verbatim* as I have related. Sir, you shall now have a ſtory of this Simon Forman, as his widow, whom I well knew, related it unto me. But before I relate his death, I shall acquaint you something of the man, as I have gathered them from some manuscripts of his own writing.

OF DR. SIMON FORMAN

He was a chandler's son in the city of Weſtminſter. He travelled into Holland for a month, in 1580, purposely to be inſtructed in aſtrology, and other more occult sciences; as also in physick, taking his degree of Doctor beyond seas: being sufficiently furnished and inſtructed with what he desired, he returned into England, towards the latter end of the reign of Queen Elizabeth, and flourished until that year of King James, wherein the Countess of Essex, the Earl of Somerset, and Sir Thomas Overbury's matters were queſtioned.[48] He lived

---

48 An intriguing moment in history surrounds Frances Howard (Countess of Essex), Robert Carr (the Earl of Somerset), and Sir Thomas Overbury (courtier and poet, and embassy of King James I). Carr and Overbury were close friends and confidants, working side by side in the service of King James I. In 1612 Carr began an illicit affair with the then-married Countess Howard, which Overbury strongly cautioned against, having suspicions of the Countess's honor and tendency to damage those who crossed her. Overbury wrote a poem, 'A Wife,' carefully laying out the attributes that a gentleman should expect from a woman before extending his hand in marriage. The Countess was introduced to the text, being

in Lambeth, with a very good report of the neighbourhood, especially of the poor, unto whom he was very charitable. He was a person that in horary questions (especially thefts) was very judicious and fortunate;[49] so

told it was a subtextual warning to Carr about his involvement with the Countess. This outraged the Countess; and in her contempt, she sought to destabilize Overbury's standing with King James I. The king was manipulated into delegating Overbury as ambassador to a Russian court. When he declined, the king was outraged and locked Overbury away in the Tower of London where he would die a mere five months later in September 1613. While jailing conditions in the seventeenth century were dismal enough to cause an inmate's death within a manner of months, suspicions of foul play circulated and eventually resulted in a trial of Howard, Carr and others thought to be involved. The trial revealed that Overbury had been poisoned. While Howard admitted to her involvement in Overbury's death, Carr did not, though both were later pardoned. Others found guilty were less fortunate and sentenced to death. The results of the trial permanently damaged James I's reputation since many felt that he was somehow involved in the plot to poison an innocent man.

Dr. Forman was implicated posthumously (having died in 1611) as being the supplier of the poison that killed Overbury, hence Lilly's assertion that Forman fell into disrepute as a result of this trial. His accusers were two of his former clients – the Countess of Essex herself, pardoned, and one Anne Turner, who was hanged for her involvement.

49 "Fortunate" here is less likely to indicate that Forman sustained a fortunate level of accuracy, but instead more likely to denote that Forman was never arraigned for divining the location of lost or stolen possessions. The Witchcraft Act of 1563 made it punishable by death to "use devise practise or exercise, or cause to be devised, practised or exercised, any Invovacons or cojuracons of Sprites, witchecraftes, enchauntementes or sorceries to thentent to fynde money or treasure [...] or by such Invovacons or cojuracons of Sprites, witchecraftes, enchauntementes or sorceries, or any of them take upon them, *to tell or declare where goodes stollen or lost shall become*" (italics mine). Though the Witchcraft Act of 1563 was repealed

also in sicknesses, which indeed was his master-piece. In resolving questions about marriage he had good success: in other questions very moderate. He was a person of indefatigable pains. I have seen sometimes half one sheet of paper wrote of his judgment upon one question;[50] in writing whereof he used much tautology,[51] as you may see yourself, (most excellent Esquire) if you read a great book of Dr. Flood's, which you have, who had all that book from the manuscripts of Forman; for I have seen the same word for word in an English manuscript formerly belonging to Doctor Willoughby of Gloucestershire. Had Forman lived to have methodized his own papers, I doubt not but he would have advanced the

---

in 1604, it was reincarnated with varying degrees of adaptation until its ultimate repeal and replacement by the Fraudulent Mediums Act of 1951.
50 Lilly was swift and concise in his taking of notes. One query Lilly left unpublished, though available on reserve at the Bodleian Library and reproduced in Parker's *Familiar to All*, is "Dns Prickman if his Mrs would live." Lilly's only note on this chart is in the center of the figure: "Shee died within a fortnight." Lilly's recorded data is Monday, 22 September 1645 (OS), or 2 October 1645 (NS), 4:45 PM LMT (though a 4:35 PM LMT calculation renders the recorded angles and house cusps).

And to the student of horary it is no wonder she passed so quickly. The eighth-ruler of the horary was Mars, shown in Libra in the seventh house, and the seventh-ruler Mercury in Scorpio conjunct the eighth house cusp, directly opposite a peregrine Saturn ruling the wife's sixth house of illness. Mercury was steadily decreasing in velocity and would soon be overtaken by Venus, the ruler of the wife's turned eighth house of death. Mercury turned retrograde soon thereafter, and met a corporal conjunction with Mars, radical eighth house ruler, on 18 October (NS), sixteen days later.
51 The same thing said twice, though in different form.

Jatro-mathematical[52] part thereof very completely; for he was very observant, and kept notes of the success of his judgments, as in many of his figures I have observed. I very well remember to have read, in one of his manuscripts, what followeth.

'Being in bed one morning,' (says he) 'I was desirous to know whether I should ever be a Lord, Earl, or Knight, &c. whereupon I set a figure; and thereupon my judgment:' by which he concluded, that within two years time he should be a Lord or great man: 'But,' says he, 'before the two years were expired, the Doctors put me in Newgate,[53] and nothing came.' Not long after, he was desirous to know the same things concerning his honour or greatship. Another figure was set, and that promised him to be a great Lord within one year. But he sets down, that in that year he had no preferment at all; only 'I became acquainted with a merchant's wife, by whom I got well.'[54] There is another figure concerning one Sir ——— Ayre his going into Turkey, whether it would be a good voyage or not: the Doctor repeats all his astrological reasons and musters them together, and then gave

---

52 More commonly spelled *iatromathematics*, from the Greek ἰατρική "medicine" and μαθηματικά "mathematics," a field of classical study that attempts to marry medicine with mathematics and astrology.

53 A prison in London. Forman was barred from medical practice by the Company of Barber-Surgeons, and was later sentenced for practicing medicine without a license after the death of one of his patients.

54 Forman was known for his voracious sexual appetite, and though he may have counted this amongst his triumphs, it was not the kind of preferment (promotion or appointment to a position or office) he envisioned as his legacy.

his judgment it would be a fortunate voyage. But under this figure he concludes, 'this proved not so, for he was taken prisoner by pirates ere he arrived in Turkey, and lost all'. He set several questions to know if he should attain the philosophers' stone, and the figures, according to his straining, did seem to signify as much; and then he tuggs upon the aspects and configurations,[55] and elected a fit time to begin his operation; but, by and by, in conclusion, he adds, 'so the work went very forward; but upon the □ of ♂ the setting-glass broke, and I lost all my pains': he sets down five or six such judgments, but still complains all came to nothing, upon the malignant aspects of ♄ and ♂. Although some of his astrological judgments did fail, more particularly those concerning himself, he being no way capable of such preferment as he ambitiously desired; yet I shall repeat some other of his judgments, which did not fail, being performed by conference with spirits. My mistress[56] went once unto him, to know when her husband, then in Cumberland, would return, he having promised to be at home near the time of the question; after some consideration, he told her to this effect: 'Margery', for so her name was, 'thy husband will not be at home these eighteen days; his kindred have vexed him, and he is come away from

---

55 To mean that Forman pulled every trick out of his pocket to back-end his way into a judgment that he preferred to find in the chart.

56 Mr. Wright's wife and Lilly's mistress. It was from Dr. Forman that Margery procured the talisman designed to protect her former husband from his nightly grazier hauntings, which Lilly sold on for thirty-two shillings after her death.

them in much anger: he is now in Carlisle, and hath but three-pence in his purse'. And when he came home he confessed all to be true, and that upon leaving his kindred he had but three-pence in his purse. I shall relate one story more, and then his death.

One Coleman, clerk to Sir Thomas Beaumont of Leicestershire, having had some liberal favours both from his lady and her daughters, bragged of it, &c. The Knight brought him into the star-chamber,[57] had his servant sentenced to be pilloried, whipped, and afterwards, during life, to be imprisoned. The sentence was executed in London, and was to be in Leicestershire: two keepers were to convey Coleman from the Fleet to Leicester. My mistress taking consideration of Coleman, and the miseries he was to suffer, went presently to Forman, acquainted him therewith; who, after consideration,[58] swore Coleman had lain both with mother and daughters; and besides said, that the old Lady being afflicted with fits of the mother, called him into her chamber to hold down the fits with his hands;[59] and that he holding

---

57 A special court designed for trying prominent persons socially or politically powerful enough to maneuver justice in ordinary courts.

58 Consider derives from the Latin *cum*, meaning "with," and *sidus/sider*, "the stars," later forming the verb *considerare* meaning "to examine." In respect to its etymology, *consideration* properly translates to "to evaluate in relation to the stars," and Lilly applies this meaning here, i.e., that Forman had drawn up an astrological chart and from it acquainted Margery with Coleman's fate.

59 Some modern sources consider "fits of the mother" to be an archaic term for strangulation of the womb, a uterine disease. Other medieval physick texts referred to as "vapours" or "hysterick disorders" what we

his hands about the breast, she cried 'Lower, lower', and put his hands below her belly; and then ————— He also told my mistress in what posture he lay with the young ladies, &c. and said, 'they intend in Leicester to whip him to death; but I assure thee, Margery, he shall never come there; yet they set forward to-morrow', says he; and so his two keepers did, Coleman's legs being locked with an iron chain under the horse's belly. In this nature they travelled the first and second day; on the third day the two keepers, seeing their prisoner's civility the two preceding days, did not lock his chain under the horse's belly as formerly, but locked it only to one side. In this posture they rode some miles beyond Northampton, when on a sudden, one of the keepers had a necessity to untruss,[60] and so the other and Coleman stood still; by and by the other keeper desired Coleman to hold his horse, for he had occasion also: Coleman immediately took one of their swords, and ran through two of the horses, killing them stark dead; gets upon the other, with one of their swords; 'Farewell, gentlemen', quoth he, 'tell my master I have no mind to be whipped in Leicestershire', and so went his way. The two keepers in all haste went to a gentleman's house near at hand, complaining of their misfortune, and desired of him to pursue their prisoner, which he with much civility granted; but ere the horses could be got ready, the mistress of

would today call epilepsy. The latter certainly seems plausible, given Forman's account of Coleman being asked to hold the Lady Beaumont down. She may have been experiencing an epileptic episode.

60 Nature does call.

the house came down, and enquiring what the matter was, went to the stable, and commanded the horses to be unsaddled, with this sharp speech – 'Let the Lady Beaumont and her daughters live honestly, none of my horses shall go forth upon this occasion'.

I could relate many such stories of his performances; as also what he wrote in a book left behind him, *viz.* 'This I made the devil write with his own hand in Lambeth Fields 1596, in June or July, as I now remember'. He professed to his wife there would be much trouble about Carr and the Countess of Essex,[61] who frequently resorted unto him, and from whose company he would sometimes lock himself in his study a whole day. Now we come to his death, which happened as follows: the Sunday night before he died, his wife and he being at supper in their garden-house, she being pleasant, told him, that she had been informed he could resolve, whether man or wife should die first; 'Whether shall I' (quoth she) 'bury you or no?' 'Oh Trunco', for so he called her, 'thou wilt bury me, but thou wilt much repent it'. 'Yea, but how long first?' 'I shall die', said he, 'ere Thursday night'. Monday came, all was well. Tuesday came, he not sick. Wednesday came, and still he was well; with which his impertinent wife did much twit him in his teeth. Thursday came, and dinner was ended, he very well: he went down to the water-side, and took a pair of oars to go to some buildings he was in hand with in Puddle-dock. Being in the middle of the Thames, he

---

61 The same Carr and Countess involved in the Overbury poisoning.

presently fell down, only saying, 'An impost, an impost', and so died.[62] A most sad storm of wind immediately following. He died worth one thousand two hundred pounds, and left only one son called Clement. All his rarities, secret manuscripts, of what quality soever, Dr. Napper of Lindford in Buckinghamshire had, who had been a long time his scholar; and of whom Forman was used to say he would be a dunce: yet in continuance of time he proved a singular astrologer and physician. Sir Richard now living, I believe, has all those rarities in possession, which were Forman's, being kinsman and heir unto Dr. Napper. [His son Thomas Napper, Esq.; most generously gave most of these manuscripts to Elias Ashmole, Esq.;] I hope you will pardon this digression.

After my mistress was dead, I lived most comfortably, my master having a great affection for me.

The year 1625 now comes on, and the plague exceeding violent, I will relate what I observed the spring before it broke forth. Against our corner house every night there would come down, about five or six of the clock, sometime one hundred or more boys, some playing, others as if in serious discourse, and just as it grew dark would all be gone home; many succeeding years there was no such, or any concourse, usually no more than four or five in a company: In the spring of 1625, the boys and youths of several parishes in like number appeared again, which I beholding, called Thomas Sanders, my landlord, and told him, that the youth and young boys

---

62 Forman's prediction of his own death.

of several parishes did in that nature assemble and play, in the beginning of the year 1625. 'God bless us', quoth I, 'from a plague this year'; but then there succeeded one, and the greateſt that ever was in London. In 1625, the visitation encreasing, and my maſter having a great charge of money and plate, some of his own, some other men's, left me and a fellow-servant to keep the house, and himself in June went into Leiceſtershire. He was in that year feoffee colleƈtor for twelve poor alms-people living in Clement-Dane's Church-Yard; whose pensions I in his absence paid weekly, to his and the parish's great satisfaƈtion. My maſter was no sooner gone down, but I bought a bass-viol, and got a maſter to inſtruƈt me; the intervals of time I spent in bowling in Lincoln's-Inn-Fields, with Wat the cobler, Dick the blacksmith, and such like companions: We have sometimes been at our work at six in the morning, and so continued till three or four in the afternoon, many times without bread or drink all that while. Sometimes I went to church and heard funeral sermons, of which there was then great plenty. At other times I went early to St. Antholine's in London, where there was every morning a sermon. The moſt able people of the whole city and suburbs were out of town; if any remained, it were such as were engaged by parish-officers to remain; no habit of a gentleman or woman continued; the woeful calamity of that year was grievous, people dying in the open fields and in open ſtreets. At laſt, in Auguſt, the bills of mortality so encreased, that very few people had thoughts of surviving the contagion: the Sunday before the great bill came forth, which was of five thousand and odd hundreds, there was appointed a sacrament at Clement Dane's; during the deſtributing whereof I do very well remember we sang thirteen parts of the one hundred and nineteenth Psalm. One Jacob, our miniſter (for we had three that day, the communion was so great) fell sick as he was giving the sacrament, went home, and was buried of the plague the Thursday following, Mr. James, another of the miniſters, fell sick ere he had quite finished, had the plague, and was thirteen weeks ere he recovered. Mr. Whitacre, the laſt of the three, escaped not only then, but all the contagion following, without any sickness at all; though he officiated at every funeral, and buried all manner of people, whether they died of the plague or not. He was given to drink, seldom could preach more than one quarter of an hour at a time, &c. In November my maſter came home. My fellow-servant's and my diet came weekly to six shillings and sixpence, sometimes to seven shillings, so cheap was diet at that time.

In February of that year, my maſter married again (one who after his death became my wife). In the same year he settled upon me, during my life, twenty pounds per annum, which I have enjoyed ever since, even to the writing hereof.

May 22, 1627, my maſter died at the corner house in the Strand, where I also lived so long. He died intestate;[63] my miſtress relinquishing the adminiſtration, it came to his elder brother, who assigned the eſtate over

---

63 Having more equity in estate to his name than enforceable debts.

to me for payment of my master's debts; which being paid, I faithfully returned the remaining part unto his administrator; nor had one penny of the estate more than twenty pounds per annum, which was allowed me by contract, to undertake the payment of my master's debts.

OF MY MARRIAGE THE FIRST TIME

My mistress, who had been twice married to old men, was now resolved to be couzened no more; she was of a brown ruddy complexion, corpulent, of but mean stature, plain, no education, yet a very provident person, and of good condition: she had many suitors, old men, whom she declined; some gentlemen of decayed fortunes, whom she liked not, for she was covetous and sparing: by my fellow-servant she was observed frequently to say, she cared not if she married a man that would love her, so that he had never a penny; and would ordinarily talk of me when she was in bed: this servant gave me encouragement to give the onset: I was much perplexed hereat, for should I attempt her, and be slighted, she would never care for me afterwards; but again, I considered that if I should attempt and fail, she would never speak of it; or would any believe I durst be so audacious as to propound such a question, the disproportion of years and fortune being so great betwixt us: however, all her talk was of husbands, and in my presence saying one day after dinner, she respected not wealth, but desired an honest man; I made answer, I thought I could fit her with such a husband; she asked me, where? I made no more ado, but presently saluted[64] her, and told her myself was the man: she replied, I was too young; I said nay; what I had not in wealth, I would supply in love; and saluted her frequently, which she accepted lovingly; and next day at dinner made me sit down at dinner with my hat on my head, and said, she intended to make me her husband; for which I gave her many salutes, &c.

I was very careful to keep all things secret, for I well knew, if she should take counsel of any friend, my hopes would be frustrated, therefore I suddenly procured her consent to marry, unto which she assented; so that upon the eighth day of September, 1627, at St. George's church in Southwark, I was married unto her, and for two whole years we kept it secret. When it was divulged, and some people blamed her for it, she constantly replied, that she had no kindred; if I proved kind, and a good husband, she would make me a man; if I proved otherwise, she only undid herself. In the third and fourth years after our marriage, we had strong suits of law with her first husband's kindred, but overthrew them in the end. During all the time of her life, which was until October, 1633, we lived very lovingly, I frequenting no company at all; my exercises were sometimes angling, in which I ever delighted: my companions, two aged men. I then frequented lectures, two or three in a week; I heard Mr.

---

64 Offering compliments and other demonstrations of respect and admiration.

Sute in Lombard-Street, Mr. Gouge of Black-Fryars, Dr. Micklethwait of the Temple, Dr. Oldsworth, with others, the most learned men of these times, and leaned in judgment to Puritanism. In October, 1627, I was made free of the Salters' company in London.

HOW I CAME TO STUDY ASTROLOGY

It happened on one Sunday, 1632, as myself and a Justice of Peace's clerk were, before service, discoursing of many things, he chanced to say, that such a person was a great scholar, nay, so learned, that he could make an Almanack, which to me then was strange: one speech begot another, till, at last, he said, he could bring me acquainted with one Evans in Gunpowder-Alley, who had formerly lived in Staffordshire, that was an excellent wise man, and studied the Black Art. The same week after we went to see Mr. Evans. When we came to his house, he, having been drunk the night before, was upon his bed, if it be lawful to call that a bed whereon he then lay;[65] he roused up himself, and, after some compliments, he was content to instruct me in astrology; I attended his best opportunities for seven or eight weeks, in which time I could set a figure perfectly: books he had not any, except

---

65 Evans was a particularly unkempt man who allowed himself and his family to live in base, slovenly conditions.

Haly de judiciis Astrorum,⁶⁶ and *Orriganus's Ephemerides*;⁶⁷ so that as often as I entered his house, I thought I was in the wilderness. Now something of the man: he was by birth a Welshman, a Master of Arts, and in sacred orders; he had formerly had a cure of souls⁶⁸ in Staffordshire, but now was come to try his fortunes at London, being in a manner enforced to fly for some offences very scandalous, committed by him in these parts, where he had lately lived; for he gave judgment upon things lost, the only shame of astrology: he was the most saturnine person my eyes ever beheld, either before I practised or since; of a middle stature; broad forehead, beetle-browed, thick shoulders, flat nosed, full lips, down-looked, black curling stiff hair, splay-footed; to give him his right, he had the most piercing judgment naturally upon a figure of theft, and many other questions, that I ever met withal; yet for money he would willingly give contrary judgments, was much addicted to debauchery, and then very abusive and quarrelsome, seldom without a black eye, or one mischief of other: this is the same Evans who made so many antimonial cups,⁶⁹ upon the sale whereof

---

66 "Haly's *Judgments of the Stars*." Haly Abenragel was a late tenth-, early eleventh-century Arabic astrologer, cited often in Lilly's *Christian Astrology* as a reliable and profound authority on the subject of judicial astrology.

67 The ephemeris of German astronomer David Origanus, who wrote a major astrological treatise published posthumously in 1645, two years before the appearance of Lilly's *Christian Astrology*.

68 A priest's exercise of his office, usually including theological instruction, the delivering of sermons, the administration of sacraments and admonitions, etc.

69 Antimonial cups held wine for the space of twenty-four hours (where

he principally subsisted; he understood Latin very well, the Greek tongue not at all: he had some arts above, and beyond astrology, for he was well versed in the nature of spirits, and had many times used the circular way of invocating, as in the time of our familiarity he told me. Two of his actions I will relate, as to me delivered. There was in Staffordshire a young gentlewoman that had, for her preferment, married an aged rich person, who was desirous to purchase some lands for his wife's maintenance; but this young gentlewoman, his wife, was desired to buy the land in the name of a gentleman, her very dear friend, but for her use: after the aged man was dead, the widow could by no means procure the deed of purchase from her friend; whereupon she applies herself to Evans, who, for a sum of money, promises to have her deed safely delivered into her own hands; the sum was forty pounds. Evans applies himself to the invocation of the angel Salmon, of the nature of Mars,[70] reads his Litany in the *Common-Prayer-Book* every day, at select hours, wears his surplice, lives orderly all that time; at the fortnight's end Salmon appeared, and having received his commands what to do, in a small time returns with the very deed desired, lays it down gently upon a table where a white cloth was spread, and then, being

the wine would interact with the metal cup and form a tartarized antimony), and were then administered. The antimonied wine would then have a purging effect, either emetic (via vomit) or purgative (via evacuation of the bowels).

70 A seemingly dangerous angel to command about, if Evans' reports are to be believed.

dismissed, vanished. The deed was, by the gentleman who formerly kept it, placed among many other of his evidences in a large wooden cheſt, and in a chamber at one end of the house; but upon Salmon's; removing and bringing away the deed, all that bay of building was quite blown down, and all his own proper evidences torn all to pieces. The second ſtory followeth.

Some time before I became acquainted with him, he then living in the Minories,[71] was desired by the Lord Bothwell and Sir Kenelm Digby[72] to show them a spirit. He promised so to do: the time came, and they were all in the body of the circle, when lo, upon a sudden, after some time of invocation, Evans was taken from out the room, and carried into the field near Battersea Causeway,[73] close to the Thames. Next morning a countryman going by to his labour, and espying a man in black cloaths, came unto him and awaked him, and asked him how he came there? Evans by this underſtood his condition, enquired where he was, how far from London, and in what parish he was; which when he underſtood, he told the labourer he had been late at Battersea the night before, and by chance was left there by his friends. Sir Kenelm Digby and the Lord Bothwell went home without any harm, and came next day to hear what was become of him; juſt as they, in the afternoon, came into the house, a messenger came from Evans to his wife,

---

71 A civil parish in London.

72 An English diplomat and courtier, esteemed as a natural philosopher.

73 This would have been some six or seven miles away.

to come to him at Battersea. I enquired upon what account the spirit carried him away: who said, he had not, at the time of invocation, made any suffumigation,⁷⁴ at which the spirits were vexed. It happened, that after I discerned what astrology was, I went weekly into Little Britain, and bought many books of astrology, not acquainting Evans therewith. Mr. A. Bedwell, Minister of Tottenham-High-Cross near London, who had been many years chaplain to Sir Henry Wotton, whilst he was Ambassador at Venice, and assisted Pietro Soave Polano, in composing and writing the Council of Trent, was lately dead; and his library being sold into Little Britain, I bought amongst them my choicest books of astrology. The occasion of our falling out was thus: a woman demanded the resolution of a question, which when he had done, she went her way; I standing by all the while, and observing the figure, asked him why he gave the judgment he did, since the signification shewed quite the contrary, and gave him my reasons; which when he had pondered, he called me boy, and must he be contradicted by such a novice! But when his heat was over, he said, had he not so judged to please the woman, she would have given him nothing, and he had a wife and family to provide for; upon this we never came together after.⁷⁵ Being now very meanly introduced, I applied

---

74 The act of providing a fume or smoke offering when invoking a celestial spirit for some magical work.
75 Lilly's self-study enabled him to see the trickery employed by Evans, which Evans employed for no other reason than to secure payment for a judgment. Lilly frequently underscored the importance of moral rectitude

myself to study those books I had obtained, many times twelve, or fifteen, or eighteen hours day and night; I was curious to discover, whether there was any verity in the art or not. Astrology in this time, *viz.* in 1633, was very rare in London, few professing it that understood any thing thereof. Let it not repent you (O noble Esquire) if now I make a short digression of such persons as then professed astrology, that posterity may understand in what condition I found it, and in whose hands that little that remained was lodged.

There lived then in Houndsditch one Alexander Hart, who had been a soldier formerly, a comely old man, of good aspect; he professed questionary astrology,[76] and a little of physick; his greatest skill was to elect young gentlemen fit times to play at dice, that they might win or get money. I went unto him for resolutions for three questions at several times, and he erred in every one. To speak soberly of him, he was but a cheat, as appeared

---

in practitioners of astrology, and often classified his contemporaries as sound or unsound based on their purity in intent and humility (though in fairness it must be said that Lilly just as often supported or diminished other astrologers as a result of their political affiliations). Later in his autobiography Lilly explains his reasoning for refusing a man's request for tutelage, saying, *"Artis est celare artem* ['It is true art to conceal art'], especially to those who live not in the fear of God, or can be masters of their own counsels." Lilly's "Letter to the Student in Astrology" still stands as an excellent moral primer for those seeking to engage seriously in the study of astrology, particularly the practice of horary astrology, and can be found in the introduction to Lilly's *Christian Astrology* published in 1647.

76 Horary astrology, often called "interrogational astrology" in the medieval period.

suddenly after; for a rustical fellow of the city, desirous of knowledge, contracted with Hart to assist for a conference with a spirit, and paid him twenty pounds of thirty pounds the contract. At last, after many delays, and no spirit appearing, or money returned, the young man indicts him for a cheat at the Old Bailey[77] in London; the Jury found the bill, and at the hearing of the cause this jest happened: some of the bench enquired what Hart did? 'He sat like an Alderman in his gown', quoth the fellow; at which the court fell into a great laughter, most of the court being Aldermen.[78] He was to have been set upon the pillory for this cheat; but John Taylour, the Water Poet, being his great friend, got the Lord Chief Justice Richardson to bail him, ere he stood upon the pillory, and so Hart fled presently into Holland, where he ended his days. It was my fortune, upon the sale of his books in 1634, to buy *Argoll's Primum Mobile* for fourteen shillings, which I only wanted.

In Lambeth Marsh at the same time lived one Captain Bubb, who resolved horary questions astrologically; a proper handsome man, well spoken, but withal covetous, and of no honesty, as will appear by this story, for which he stood upon the pillory. A certain butcher was robbed, going to a fair, of forty pounds; he goes to Bubb, who for ten pounds in hand paid, would help him to the thief; appoints the butcher such a night precise-

---

77 The central court of London.

78 An elected member of a municipal council. It was customary for aldermen to wear gowns. This comment implies that Hart gave false pretense of celestial knowledge and sought to defraud the plaintiff.

ly, to watch at such a place, and the thief should come thither; commanded him by any means to stop him; the butcher attends according to direction. About twelve in the night there comes one riding very fiercely upon a full gallop, whom the butcher knocks down, and seized both upon man and horse: the butcher brings the man and horse to the next town, but then the person whom the butcher attacked was John the servant of Dr. Bubb; for which the Captain was indicted and suffered upon the pillory, and afterwards ended his days in great disgrace.

There was also one Jeffry Neve, at this time a student in physic and astrology; he had formerly been a merchant in Yarmouth,[79] and Mayor of the town, but failing in estate, went into the Low-Countries,[80] and at Franecker[81] took the degree of Doctor in Physick; he had some little smattering in astrology; could resolve a question of theft, or love-question, something of sickness; a very grave person, laborious and honest, of tall stature and comely feature; he died of late years, almost in the very street near Tower-Hill: he had a design of printing two hundred verified questions, and desired my approbation ere they went to press; that I first would see them, and then give testimony. When I had perused the first forty, I corrected thirty of them, would read over no more: I showed him how erroneous they were, desired his emendation of the rest, which he performed

---

79 A coastal town approximately 125 miles northeast of London.
80 Those countries forming the northwestern coastline of Europe.
81 A city in Holland.

not. These were afterwards, in R. Saunders's[82] custody, bought by him either of his son or of a stationer.*

There was then William Poole, a nibbler at astrology, sometimes a gardener, an apparitor, a drawer of linen; as quoifs, handkerchiefs; a plaisterer and a bricklayer; he would brag many times he had been of seventeen professions; was very good company for drolling, as you yourself very well remember (most honoured Sir);† he pretended to poetry; and that posterity may have a taste of it, you shall have here inserted two verses of his own making; the occasion of making them was thus. One Sir Thomas Jay, a Justice of the Peace in Rosemary-Lane, issued out his warrant for the apprehension of Poole, upon a pretended suggestion, that he was in company

* But first offered to be sold to me for twenty shillings. When Mr. Saunders died I bought them of his son for less. E. A----.[83]

† December 17, this William Poole was married to Alice How, at St. George's Church in Southwark. Mr. Lilly gave her to him.

---

82 Richard Saunders. Near the end of his life, Lilly wrote an introduction to Saunders' medical text, *Astrological Judgement and Practice of Physicke* (1677).

83 Lilly wrote the autobiography of his life to close friend and confidant Elias Ashmole, and Ashmole is frequently addressed within its pages ("most honoured Sir," "oh learned Esquire," etc.). When the manuscript was originally published in 1715, Ashmole's footnotes were included, Ashmole also wrote the closing paragraphs of the autobiography to fill in information regarding Lilly's death and the epitaphs left in his wake.

with some lewd people in a tavern, where a silver cup was lost, *Anglice* stolen. Poole, hearing of the warrant, packs up his little trunk of books, being all his library, and runs to Westminster; but hearing some months after that the Justice was dead and buried, he came and enquired where the grave was; and after the discharge of his belly upon the grave, left these two verses upon it, which he swore he made himself.

> *Here lieth buried Sir Thomas Jay, Knight,*
> *Who being dead, I upon his grave did shite.*

He died about 1651, or 1652, at St. Mary Overy's in Southwark; and this was part of his last will.

'Item; I give to Dr. Ardee all my books, and one manuscript of my own, worth one hundred of Lilly's Introduction'.[84]

'Item; If Dr. Ardee give my wife any thing that is mine, I wish the devil may fetch him body and soul'. The Doctor, terrified with this curse, gave me all the books and his goods which I presently gave to his widow.———*Interdum seria jocis.*[85]

Now also lived this Dr. Ardee, but his true name was Richard Delahay, formerly an Attorney; he studied astrology and physick, being in necessity, and forced from Derbyshire, where he had lived, by the old Countess

---

84 Lilly's "*Christian Astrology, modestly treated of in three books...*" (1647) was often called, by himself and others, Lilly's "Introduction."

85 Rough colloquial translation, "Now and then we have our jokes."

of Shrewsbury; he was of moderate judgment, both in astrology and physick. He had formerly been well acquainted with Charles Sledd,* an apothecary, who used the crystal, and had a very perfect sight. This Dr. Ardee hath many times affirmed unto me, (*esto fides*)[86] that an angel, one time, appeared unto him, and offered him a lease of his life for one thousand years; he died about the age of fourscore years; left his widow, who married into Kent,† worth two or three thousand pounds, and William Poole's estate came to four or five pounds.

In the years 1632 and 1633, John Booker became famous for a prediction of his upon a solar eclipse in the 19th degree of Aries 1663, taken out of *Leovitius de magnis conjunctionibus*, viz. *Oh Reges et Principes &c.* Both the King of Bohemia, and Gustavus King of Sweden, dying during the effects of that eclipse.

John Booker was born in Manchester, of good parentage, in the year 1601; was in his youth well instructed in the Latin tongue, which he understood very well.

He seemed from his infancy to be designed for astrology; for from the time he had any understanding, he would be always poring on, and studying almanacks. He came to London at fitting years, and served an apprenticeship to an haberdasher in Laurence-Lane, London;

* Of this Charles Sledd, there is mention made in Dr. Dee's book of his discourse with spirits, set forth by Dr. Casaubon.
† To one Moreland.

---

86 "This you may trust," a cheeky comment considering what follows.

but either wanting stock to set up, or disliking the calling, he left his trade, and taught to write at Hadley in Middlesex several scholars in that school: he wrote singularly well both Secretary[87] and Roman.[88] In process of time he served Sir Christopher Clethero, Knight, Alderman of London, as his clerk, being a city Justice of Peace: he also was clerk to Sir Hugh Hammersley, Alderman of London, both which he served with great credit and estimation; and by that means became not only well known, but as well respected of the most eminent citizens of London, even to his dying day.

He was an excellent proficient in astrology, whose excellent verses upon the twelve months,[89] framed according to the configurations of each month, being blessed with success according to his predictions, procured him much reputation all over England: he was a very honest man, abhorred any deceit in the art he studied; had a curious fancy in judging of thefts, and as successful in resolving love-questions: he was no mean proficient in astronomy; he understood much of physick; was a great admirer of the antimonial cup; not unlearned in chymistry, which he loved well, but did not practise. He was inclined to a diabetes; and in the last three years of his life was afflicted with a dysentery, which at last consumed him to nothing: he died of good fame in 1667. Since his decease I have seen one nativity of his perfor-

---

87 A formal style of handwriting, common in early modern England and Germany.

88 Print (as opposed to cursive, or secretary).

89 Booker's almanacs.

JOHN BOOKER

From a Rare Print by Hollar

mance exactly directed, and judged with as much learning as from astrology can be expected.

His library of books came short of the world's approbation, and were by his widow sold to Elias Ashmole, Esq. who most generously gave her* far more money than they were worth;[90] but out of his respects unto the deceased and his memory, he most willingly paid her the money. He left behind him two sons and two daughters. He left in writing very little but his annual prognostications. He began first to write about the year 1630; he wrote *Bellum Hibernicale*,[91] in the time of the long parliament,[92] a very sober and judicious book: the epistle thereunto I gave him. He wrote lately a small treatise of Easter-Day, a very learned thing, wherein he shewed much learning and reading. To say no more of him, he lived an honest man, his fame not questioned at his death.

In this year 1633, I became acquainted with Nicholas Fiske,[93] licentiate in physick, who was born in Suffolk,

* They cost me one hundred and forty pounds.

---

90 It was noted in Booker's will that his library should be sold to Ashmole if he paid Booker's widow a sum of £140 and no less.
91 A variant, *Bellum Hibernica*, translates to "Irish War."
92 Established in 1640, the Long Parliament was so named because, through an Act of Parliament, it could not be dissolved without the consent of its members. It was not dissolved fully (though there were disruptions) until 1660, after the end of the Civil War and within months of the Restoration that reinstated the English monarchy.
93 John Gadbury's teacher.

near Framingham* Castle, of very good parentage, who educated him at country schools, until he was fit for the university; but he went not to the academy, studying at home both astrology and physick, which he afterwards practised in Colchester; and there was well acquainted with Dr. Gilbert, who wrote *De Magnete*.[94] He came afterwards unto London, and exercised his faculty in several places thereof. (For in his youth he would never stay long in one house.) In 1633 he was sent for out of Suffolk by Dr. Winston of Gresham College, to instruct the Lord Treasurer Weston's son in arithmetick, astronomy upon the globes, and their uses. He was a person very

* There is no such place in Suffolk, it being mistaken for Framlingham in that county.

---

94 The full title is given out as, *De Magnete, Magneticisque Corporibus, et de Magno Magnete Tellure*, or "On the Magnet and Magnetic Bodies, and On That Great Magnet the Earth," published in 1600 by Dr. William Gilbert, physick and scientist. This work was profoundly influential for its time. In it, Gilbert explained why compasses point north (i.e., the earth was magnetic – prior to this it was believed that Polaris, the North Star, attracted the needle of a compass; Gilbert even explains why there is variation in how accurate compasses are in pointing north). He expounded upon his studies of static electricity produced by amber (whose name is *elektron* in Greek and *electrum* in Latin) and named the phenomenon *electricus* (the origin of the modern terms "electric" and "electricity"). He ends his treatise with a fascinating argument for the Copernican model of the solar system, questioning how could we postulate that the distant sphere of the fixed stars rotated about the earth in twenty-four hours. Surely, to Gilbert, it was more logical to say the earth was doing the rotating.

studious, laborious, of good apprehension, and had by his own industry obtained both in astrology, physick, arithmetick, astronomy, geometry and algebra, singular judgment: he would in astrology resolve horary questions very soundly; but was ever diffident of his own abilities: he was exquisitely skilful in the art of directions upon nativities, and had a good genius in performing judgment thereupon, but very unhappy he was, that he had no genius in teaching his scholars, for he never perfected any: his own son Matthew hath often told me, that where his father did teach any scholars in his time, they would principally learn of him; he had Scorpio ascending, and was secretly envious to those he thought had more parts than himself; however, I must be ingenuous, and do affirm, that by frequent conversation with him, I came to know which were the best authors, and much to enlarge my judgment, especially in the art of directions:[95] he visited me most days once after I became acquainted with him, and would communicate his most doubtful questions unto me, and accept of my judgment therein rather than his own: he singularly well judged and directed Sir Robert Holborn's nativity, but desired me to adjudge the first house, seventh and tenth thereof, which I did, and which nativity (since Sir Robert gave it me) came to your hands, and remains in your library;

---

95 Lilly explains in his third book of *Christian Astrology* that the study of directions was particularly perplexing for him, and as a result he took great care in passing down his understanding of the mathematics involved. It is still one of the best resources available for understanding the calculations of primary directions.

[oh learned Esquire!] he died about the seventy-eighth year of his age, poor.

In this year also William Bredon, parson or vicar of Thornton in Buckinghamshire, was living, a profound divine, but absolutely the most polite[96] person for nativities in that age, strictly adhering to Ptolemy, which he well understood; he had a hand in composing Sir Christopher Heydon's *Defence of Judicial Astrology*,[97] being that time his chaplain; he was so given over to tobacco and drink, that when he had no tobacco, he would cut the bell-ropes and smoke them.

I come now to continue the story of my own life, but thought it not inconvenient to commit unto memory something concerning those persons who practised when first I became a student in astrology; I have wrote nothing concerning any of them, which I myself do not either know, or believe to be true.

In October 1633 my first wife died, and left me whatever was hers: it was considerable, very near to the value of one thousand pounds.

---

96 Accomplished, refined, sophisticated in judgment.
97 Heydon's *Defence*, published in 1603, was a calculated response to *A Treatise Against Judiciall Astrologie* by John Chamber (1601), which implored Parliament to outlaw judicial astrology. Heydon wrote, but did not publish, *An Astrological Discourse with Mathematical Demonstrations*, at some time in the first decade of the seventeenth century. This was an additional rebuttal of the 1601 *Treatise*, containing references to the works of Johannes Kepler and observations on the 1603 Saturn/Jupiter conjunction. Fiske inherited the work but was unsuccessful in publishing. Elias Ashmole eventually edited and published the work in 1650 with a preface from Lilly.

One whole year and more I continued a widower, and followed my studies very hard; during which time a scholar pawned unto me, for forty shillings, *Ars Notoria*,*[98] a large volume wrote in parchment, with the names of those angels, and their pictures, which are thought and believed by wise men, to teach and instruct in all the several liberal sciences, and is attained by observing elected times, and those prayers appropriated unto the several angels.

I do ingenuously acknowledge, I used those prayers according to the form and direction prescribed for some weeks, using the word *astrologia* for *astronomia*; but of this no more: that *Ars Notoria*, inserted in the latter end of Cornelius Agrippa[99] signifieth nothing; many of the prayers being not the same, nor is the direction to these prayers any thing considerable.

In the year 1634, I taught Sir George Peckham, Knight, astrology, that part which concerns sickness, wherein he so profited, that in two or three months he would give a very true discovery of any disease, only by his figures. He practised in Nottingham, but unfortunately died in 1635, at St. Winifred's Well in Wales; in

* Among Dr. Napier's[100] MSS. I had an *Ars Notoria*, written by S. Forman in large vellum.

---

98 "Art of Magic."

99 Late fifteenth-, early sixteenth-century German author of the *Three Books of Occult Philosophy*.

100 Richard Napier, English clergyman and student of Simon Forman. His casebooks are available in the Bodleian Library in Oxford.

which well he continued so long mumbling his *Pater Nosters* and *Sancta Winifrida ora pro me*,[101] that the cold struck into his body; and, after his coming forth of that well, never spoke more.

In this year 1634, I purchased the moiety of thirteen houses in the Strand for five hundred and thirty pounds.[102]

In November, the 18th day, I was again the second time married, and had five hundred pounds portion with that wife; she was of the nature of Mars.[103]

Two accidents happened to me in that year something memorable.

Davy Ramsey, his Majesty's clock-maker, had been

---

101 "Our Fathers," and "Saint Winifred, Pray For Me" – prayers.
102 The details of this transaction are explored astrologically in Lilly's chart judgment for "If I should purchase Master B., his houses" in *Christian Astrology* (219–22). Lilly comments,

The truth of the matter is, I had a hard bargain, as the Figure every way considered does manifest, and shall never live to see many of the leases yet in being, expired: and as Venus is in Aries, viz. opposite to her own House, so did I myself injury by the Bargain, I mean in matter of Money; but the love I bore to the House I now live in, wherein I lived happily with a good Master full seven years, and therein obtained my first Wife, and was bountifully blessed by God with the Goods of this World therein, made me neglect a small hindrance, nor now, I thank God, do I repent it; finding God's blessing in a plentiful measure upon my Labours. (222)

Despite this transaction's difficulty, this surely must have been a proud and life-affirming moment for Lilly, the son of a country farmer, said by the same to be "good for nothing," coming to London as a lowly servant to write and fetch water from the Thames for his master's bath.
103 This martial woman's name was Jane.

informed, that there was a great quantity of treasure buried in the cloyster of Westminster-Abbey; he acquaints Dean Williams therewith, who was also then Bishop of Lincoln; the Dean gave him liberty to search after it, with this proviso, that if any was discovered, his church should have a share of it. Davy Ramsey finds out one John Scott,* who pretended the use of the Mosaical rods,[104] to assist him herein: I was desired to join with him, unto which I consented. One winter's night, Davy Ramsey, with several gentlemen, myself, and Scott, entered the cloysters; we played the hazel-rod round about the cloyster; upon the west-side of the cloysters the rods turned one over another, an argument that the treasure was there. The labourers digged at least six foot deep, and then we met with a coffin; but in regard it was not heavy, we did not open, which we afterwards much repented. From the cloysters we went into the Abbey church, where, upon a sudden, (there being no wind when we began) so fierce, so high, so blustering and loud a wind did rise, that we verily believed the west-end of the church would have fallen upon us; our rods would not move at all; the candles and torches, all but one, were extinguished, or burned very

* This Scott lived in Pudding-Lane, and had some time been a page (or such like) to the Lord Norris.

---

104 A divining rod used to uncover the location of buried treasure. Historically these have also been used to find underground sources of water (dowsing), or to find metals and other resources.

dimly.* John Scott, my partner, was amazed, looked pale, knew not what to think or do, until I gave directions and command to dismiss the dæmons; which when done, all was quiet again, and each man returned unto his lodging late, about twelve o'clock at night; I could never since be induced to join with any in such-like actions.

The true miscarriage of the business, was by reason of so many people being present at the operation; for there was about thirty, some laughing, others deriding us; so that if we had not dismissed the dæmons, I believe most part of the Abbey church had been blown down; secrecy and intelligent operators, with a strong confidence and knowledge of what they are doing, are best for this work.

In 1634, or 1635, a Lady living in Greenwich, who had tried all the known artists in London, but to no purpose, came weeping and lamenting her condition, which was this: she had permitted a young Lord to have the use of her body, till she was with child by him; after which time he could not or would not endure her sight, but commanded his lacquies and servants to keep his doors fast shut, lest she should get into his chamber; or if they chanced to see her near his lodging, to drive her away, which they several times had done. Her desire unto me was to assist her to see him, and then she should be content; whereupon I ordered, such a day, such an hour of that day, to try her fortune once more. She obeyed; and when she came to the King's Bench, where the Lord

* Davy Ramsey brought an half quartern sack to put the treasure in.

there was imprisoned, the outward door stood wide open: none speaking a word unto her, she went up stairs, no body molesting her; she found the Lord's chamber door wide open: he in bed, not a servant to be heard or seen, so she was pleased. Three days after she came to acquaint me with her success, and then drew out of her pocket a paper full of ratsbane,[105] which, had she not had admission unto him that day I appointed, she would in a pint of white wine have drank at the stair's foot where the Lord lodged. The like misfortune befell her after that; when the Lord was out of prison: then I ordered her such a day to go and see a play at Salisbury-Court; which she did, and within one quarter of an hour the Lord came into the same box wherein she was. But I grew weary of such employments, and since have burned my books which instructed these curiosities: for after that I became melancholy, very much afflicted with the hypochondriack,[106] growing lean and spare, and every day worse; so that in the year 1635 my infirmity continuing, and my acquaintance increasing, I resolved to live in the country, and in March and April 1636 removed my goods unto Hersham, where I now live;[107] and in May

---

105 Rat poison.

106 In the medieval period, hypochondria was said to lodge itself as a despairing condition in the upper part of the abdomen.

107 Lilly makes a connection between his deteriorating health, and the subsequent decision to burn his magical texts and refrain from any further magical involvement. It may be that Lilly believed the cause of his health troubles stemmed from his forays into magic and associating with those who invoke spirits. Lilly later notes that his health did steadily pick up after

my person, where I continued until 1641, no notice being taken who, or what I was.

In the years 1637 and 1638, I had great lawsuits both in the Exchequer and Chancery, about a lease I had of the annual value of eighty pounds: I got the victory.

In the year 1640 I instructed John Humphreys, master of that art, in the study of astrology: upon this occasion, being at London, by accident in Fleet-Street, I met Dr. Percival Willoughby of Derby; we were of old acquaintance, and he but by great chance lately come to town, we went to the Mitre-Tavern in Fleet-Street, where I sent for old Will Poole the astrologer, living then in Ram-Alley: being come to us, the Doctor produced a bill,[108] set forth by a master of arts in Cambridge, intimating his abilities for resolving of all manner of questions astrologically. The bill was shewed, and I wondering at it Poole made answer, he knew the man, and that he was a silly fool; 'I', quoth he, 'can do more than he; he sees me every day, he will be here by and by'; and indeed he came into our room presently: Poole had, just as we came to him, set a figure, and then shewed it me, desiring my judgement; which I refused, but desired the master of arts to judge first; he denied, so I gave mine, to the very great liking of Humphreys, who presently enquired, if I would teach him, and for what? I told him I was willing to teach, but would have one hundred pounds. I heard

he removed himself to the countryside, and it appears from his autobiography (and contemporary accounts) that Lilly would not experiment with magical incredibilia again in his lifetime.
108 An advertisement.

Poole, whilst I was judging the figure, whisper in Humphrey's ear, and swear I was the best in England. Staying three or four days in town, at last we contracted for forty pounds, for I could never be quiet from his solicitations; he invited me to supper, and before I had shewed him any thing, paid me thirty-five pounds. As we were at supper a client came to speak with him, and so up into his closet he went with his client; I called him in before he set his figure, or resolved the question, and instantly acquainted him how he should discover the moles or marks of his client: he set his figure, and presently discovers four moles the querent had; and was so overjoyed therewith, that he came tumbling down the stairs, crying, 'Four by G—, four by G—, I will not take one hundred pounds for this one rule'. In six weeks time, and tarrying with him three days in a week, he became a most judicious person.

This Humphreys was a laborious person, vain-glorious, loquacious, fool-hardy, desirous of all secrets which he knew not, insomuch that he would have given me two hundred pounds to have instructed him in some curiosities he was persuaded I had knowledge of, but, *Artis est celare artem*,[109] especially to those who live not in the fear of God, or can be masters of their own counsels: he was in person and condition such another as that monster of ingratitude my *quondam*[110] taylor, John Gadbury.[111]

---

109 "It is true art to conceal art."

110 "Former."

111 Gadbury was an early defender of Lilly, but for personal and political reasons (Gadbury was a fervent Royalist) the two became estranged,

After my refusal of teaching him, what he was not capable of, we grew strange, though I afforded him many civilities whenever he required it; for after the siege of Colchester he wrote a book against me, called *Anti Merlinus-Anglicus*,[112] married a second wife, his first living in Cambridgeshire, then practised physick by a contrary name, having intentions to practise in Ireland; he went to Bristol, but there understanding the parliament's forces had reduced that kingdom, he came back to London, but durst not abide therein; but turning from his second wife, who also had another husband, he went to sea, with intention for Barbadoes, but died by the way in his voyage. I had never seen John Booker at that time; and telling him one day I had a desire to see him, but first, ere I would speak with him, I would fit myself with

---

bitter rivals. So intense was their dispute that they would each publish whole volumes simply for the sake of undercutting the other. Some of the more humorous attacks came when Lilly suggested that Gadbury must be something of a cheat, a liar, an amibitous and false lecher, and a jealous degenerate, all for the terrible crime of being born under a Scorpio ascendant. This enraged Gadbury (to Lilly's great delight and amusement), and the two went back and forth on this one topic in many volumes, one responding and one defending. One particularly delightful title in this heated exchange comes from Gadbury's short book dedicated to the subject: "Obsequium Rationabile; or, a reasonable service performed to the coelestial sign Scorpio; in xx. remarkable genitures of that glorious, but stigmatized horoscope: against the malitious ... attempts of that grand (but fortunate) imposter, Mr. W. Lilly" (London, 1675).

112 Lilly's almanacs went by the name of *Merlinus Anglicus*, or "The English Merlin." *Anti Merlinus-Anglicus* was one of many published attempts by Lilly's contemporaries to discredit him and expose him as fraudulent.

my old rules, and rub up my astrology; for at that time [and this was 1640] I thought John Booker the greatest and most complete astrologer in the world. My scholar Humphreys presently made answer, 'Tutor, you need not pump for any of your former knowledge, John Booker is no such pumper; we met', saith he, 'the other day, and I was too hard for him myself, upon judgment of three or four questions'. If all the transactions happening unto that my scholar were in one volume, they would transcend either *Guzman*, *Don Quixote*, *Lazarillo de Tormes*, or any other of the like nature I ever did see.

Having now in part recovered my health, being weary of the country, and perceiving there was money to be got in London, and thinking myself to be as sufficiently enabled in astrology as any I could meet with, I made it my business to repair thither; and so in September 1641 I did; where, in the years 1642 and 1643, I had great leisure to better my former knowledge: I then read over all my books of astrology, over and over; had very little or no practice at all: and whereas formerly I could never endure to read *Valentine Naibod's Commentary upon Alcabitius*, now having seriously studied him, I found him to be the profoundest author I ever met with; him I traversed over day and night, from whom I must acknowledge to have advanced my judgment and knowledge unto that height I soon after arrived at, or unto: a most rational author, and the sharpest expositor of *Ptolemy* that hath yet appeared. To exercise my genius, I began to collect notes, and thought of writing some little thing upon the ☌ of ♄ and ♃ then approaching: I had not wrote above one sheet, and that very meanly, but James Lord Galloway came to see me; and, by chance, casting his eyes upon that rude collection, he read it over, and so approved of it, yea, so encouraged me to proceed farther, that then, and after that time, I spent most of my time in composing thereof, and bringing it, in the end, into that method wherein it was printed 1644.[113] I do seriously now profess, I had not the assistance of any person living, in the writing or composing thereof. Mr. Fiske sent me a small manuscript, which had been Sir Christopher Heydon's, who had wrote something of the conjunction of ♄ and ♃, 1603; out of which, to bring my method in order, I transcribed, in the beginning, five or six lines, and not any more, though that graceless fellow Gadbury wrote the contrary: but, *Semel et semper nebulo et mendax.*[114] I did formerly write one treatise, in the year 1639, upon the eclipse of the sun, in the eleventh degree of Gemini, May 22, 1639; it consisted of six sheets of paper. But that manuscript I gave unto my most munificent patron and ever bountiful friend, William Pennington, of Muncaster in Cumberland, Esq., a wise and excellently learned person; who, from the year 1634, even till he died, continued unto me the most grateful person I ever was acquainted with. I became acquainted with him by means of Davy Ramsey.

Oh! most noble Esquire, let me now beg your pardon,

---

113 Notes on this conjunction were published in both England's *Prophetical Merlin*, and Lilly's *Merlinus Anglicus Junior* for 1644. These were to be the first of his annual almanacs.

114 "Once and always the clown and liar."

if I digress for some small time, in commemorating his bounty unto me, and my requital of his friendship, by performing many things successfully for his advantage.

In 1639 he was made captain, and served his Majesty in his then wars against the Scots; during which time a farmer's daughter being delivered of a bastard, and hearing, by report, that he was slain, fathered the child upon him. Shortly after he returned, most woefully vexed to be thus abused, when absent. The woman was countenanced by some gentlemen of Cumberland, in this her villany against him; so that, notwithstanding he had warrants to attach her body, he could never discover her: but yet, hunting her from one place to another, her friends thought it most convenient to send her to London, where she might be in most safety. She came up to the city, and immediately I had notice thereof, and the care of that matter was left unto me. I procured the Lord Chief Justice Bramston's warrant, and had it lying dormant by me. She had not been in the city above one fortnight, but that I, going casually to the clerk of the assizes' office[115] for Cumberland, saw there an handsome woman; and hearing of her speak the northern tone, I concluded she was the party I did so want. I rounded the clerk in his ear, and told him I would give him five shillings to hold the woman in chat till I came again, for I had a writing concerned her. I hasted for my warrant, and a constable, and returned into the office, seized

---

115 A county court that held frequent sessions to hear civil and criminal cases.

her person before the clerk of the assizes, who was very angry with me: it was then sessions at Old-Bayley, and neither Judge nor Justice to be found. At night we carried her before the Recorder, Gardner. It being Saturday at night, she, having no bail, was sent to Bridewell, where she remained till Monday. On Monday morning, at the Old-Bayley, she produced bail; but I desiring of the Recorder some time to enquire after the bail, whether they were sufficient, returned presently, and told him one of the bail was a prisoner in Ludgate, the other a very poor man. At which he was so vexed, that he sent her to Newgate, where she lay all that week, until she could please me with good sureties; which then she did, and so was bound over to appear at the next assizes in Cumberland; which she did, and was there sentenced to be whipped, and imprisoned one whole year.

This action infinitely pleased Mr. Pennington, who thought I could do wonders; and I was most thankfully requited for it.[116] All the while of this scandalous

---

[116] From Philip Graves: "We acquire clear insights into Lilly's mind through his own voice. While his pride at having assisted his friend William Pennington in rounding up a fugitive woman who had supposedly slighted Pennington by becoming pregnant by another man does not hold Lilly in high esteem to modern sensibilities regarding the rights of women, it has to be understood in the context of the social mores of his time in which male friends were fiercely loyal to each other's reputations and interests. And it is surely when we witness the care and attention with which Lilly treated the sick and the poor, including those suffering from the highly contagious plague, and the free giving of his time and astrological advice to those too poor to pay him, that we come to admire him the most as a man. There are also laudable examples of his freely giving of his

business, do what he could, he could not discover what persons they were that supported her; but the woman's father coming to town, I became acquainted with him, by the name of Mr. Sute, merchant; invited him to a dinner; got George Farmer with me; when we so plied him with wine, he could neither see or feel. I paid the reckoning, twenty-two shillings. But next morning the poor man had never a writing or letter in his pocket. I sent them down to my friend, who thereby discovered the plots of several gentlemen in the business; after which, Mr. Sute returned to his old name again.

Mr. Pennington was a true royalist, whom Charles the Second made one of his Commissioners of Array[117] for Cumberland. Having directions from me continually how matters did and would go betwixt the King and Parliament, he acted warily, and did but sign one only warrant of that nature, and then gave over. When the times of sequestrations[118] came, one John Musgrave, the most bold and impudent fellow, and most active of all the north of England, and most malicious against my friend, had got this warrant under Mr. Pennington's hand into his custody; which affrighted my friend, and so it might, for it was cause enough of sequestration, and

---

considerable fortune to good causes, and exercising clemency towards his erstwhile antagonists such as arch-Royalist astrologer George Wharton when the latter is being persecuted by an unjust third-party prosecution."

117 A Commissioner of Array kept the territory he oversaw (in Mr. Pennington's case, Cumberland) conditioned and prepared for war, or other forms of military service.

118 The seizing of property for state control.

CHARLES THE SECOND

*From a Picture in the Collection of the
Dutchess of Dorset at Knowle*

would have done it. Musgrave intending himself great matters out of his estate, I was made acquainted herewith. Musgrave being in London, by much ado, I got acquainted with him, pretending myself a bitter enemy against Pennington, whereat he very heartily rejoiced; and so we appointed one night to meet at the Five Bells, to compare notes; for I pretended much. We did meet, and he very suddenly produced upon the table all his papers, and withal, the warrant of array unto which my friend had set his hand; which when I saw, 'I marry', said I, 'this is his hand I will swear; now have at all come, the other cup, this warrant shall pay for all'. I observed where the warrant lay upon the table, and, after some time took occasion ignorantly to let the candle fall out, which whilst he went to light again at the fire, I made sure of the warrant, and put it into my boot; he never missing it of eight or ten days; about which time, I believe, it was above half way towards Cumberland, for I instantly sent it by the post, with this friendly caveat, '*Sin no more*'. Musgrave durst not challenge me in those times, and so the business was ended very satisfactory to his friend, and no less to myself.

He was, besides, extremely abused by one Isaac Antrobus, parson[119] of Egremond, a most evil liver, bold, and very rich; at last he procured a minister of that country, in hope of the parsonage, to article against him in London, before the committee of plundered ministers. I was once more invited to solicit against Antrobus, which

---

119 A priest of an independent Church in the pre-Reformation period.

I did upon three or more articles.

I. That Antrobus baptized a cock, and called him Peter.

II. He had knowledge of such a woman and of her daughter, *viz.* of both their bodies, in as large a manner as ever of his own wife.

III. Being drunk, a woman took a cord and tied it about his privy members unto a manger in a stable.

IV. Being a continual drunkard.

V. He never preached, &c.

Antrobus was now become a great champion for the Parliament; but, at the day of hearing, I had procured abundance of my friends to be there; for the godly, as they termed themselves, sided with him; the present Master of the Rolls was Chairman that day, Sir Harbottle Grimston.

Who, hearing the foulness of the cause, was very much ashamed thereof. I remember Antrobus, being there, pleaded he was in his natural condition[120] when he acted so ungraciously.

'What condition were you in', said the Chairman, 'when you lay with mother and daughter?'

'There is no proof of that', saith he.

'None but your own confession', said the Chairman, 'nor could any tell so well'.

'I am not given to drunkenness', quoth he. 'He was

---

120 Sober and aware of his own actions.

so drunk within this fortnight', quoth I, 'he reeled from one side of the street to the other; here is the witness to prove it:' who, presently, before the committee, being sworn, made it good, and named the place and street where he was drunk. So he was adjudged scandalous, and outed of his benefice, and our minister had the parsonage.

You cannot imagine how much the routing of this drunken parson pleased Mr. Pennington, who paid all charges munificently and thankfully.

But now follows the last and greatest kindness I ever did him. Notwithstanding the committee for sequestrations in Cumberland were his very good friends, yet the sub-sequestrators, of their own heads, and without order, and by strength of arms, secured his irons, his wood, and so much of his personal estate as was valued at seven thousand pounds. Now had I complaint upon complaint: would I suffer my old friend to be thus abused? it was in my power to free him from these villains.

I hereupon advised what was best to do, and was counselled to get Mr. Speaker Lenthall's[121] letter to the sub-sequestrators, and command them to be obedient to the committee of the county.

Whereupon, I framed a letter myself, unto the sub-sequestrators directed, and with it, myself and Mr. Laurence Maydwell (whom yourself well knew) went to Mr. Speaker, unto whom we sufficiently related the

---

121 William Lenthall, Speaker of the House of Commons.

stubbornness of the officers of Cumberland; their disobedience to the committee; and then shewed him the letter, which when he had read over, he most courteously signed, adding withal, that if they proceeded further in sequestring Mr. Pennington, he would command a Serjeant at Arms to bring them up to answer their contempts: I immediately posted that letter to my friend, which when the absurd fellows received, they delivered him possession of his goods again; and, for my pains, when he came to London, gave me one hundred pounds; he died in 1652, of a violent fever. I did carefully, in 1642 and 1643, take notice of every grand action which happened betwixt King and Parliament, and did first then incline to believe, that as all sublunary affairs[122] did depend upon superior causes, so there was a possibility of discovering them by the configurations of the superior bodies; in which way making some essays in those two years, I found encouragement to proceed further, which I did; I perused the writings of the ancients, but therein they were silent, or gave no satisfaction; at last, I framed unto myself that method, which then and since I follow, which, I hope, in time may be more perfected by a more penetrating person than myself.

In 1643, I became familiarly known to Sir Bulstrode Whitlocke, a member of the House of Commons; he being sick, his urine was brought unto me by

---

122 Terrestrial.

Mrs. Lisle,* wife to John Lisle, afterwards one of the keepers of the Great Seal; having set my figure, I returned answer, the sick for that time would recover, but by means of a surfeit would dangerously relapse within one month; which he did, by eating of trouts at Mr. Sand's house, near Leatherhead in Surrey. Then I went daily to visit him, Dr. Prideau despairing of his life; but I said there was no danger thereof, and that he would be sufficiently well in five or six weeks; and so he was.

In 1644, I published *Merlinus Anglicus Junior* about April. I had given one day the copy thereof unto the then Mr. Whitlocke, who by accident was reading thereof in the House of Commons: ere the Speaker took the chair, one looked upon it, and so did many, and got copies thereof; which when I heard, I applied myself to John Booker to license it, for then he was licenser of all mathematical books; I had, to my knowledge, never seen him before; he wondered at the book, made many impertinent obliterations, framed many objections, swore it was not possible to distinguish betwixt King and Parliament; at last licensed it according to

---

* She was afterwards beheaded at Winchester, for harbouring one Nelthrop, a rebel in the Duke of Monmouth's army 1685. She had made herself remarkable, by saying at the martyrdom of King Charles I, 1648, 'that her blood leaped within her to see the tyrant fall'; for this, when she fell into the state trap, she neither did nor could expect favour from any of that martyr's family.

his own fancy;[123] I delivered it unto the printer, who being an arch Presbyterian, had five of the ministry to inspect it, who could make nothing of it, but said it might be printed, for in that I meddled not with their Dagon.[124] The first impression was sold in less than one week; when I presented some to the members of Parliament, I complained of John Booker the licenser, who had defaced my book; they gave me order forthwith to reprint it as I would, and let them know if any durst resist me in the reprinting, or adding what I thought fit; so the second time it came forth as I would have it.

I must confess, I now found my scholar Humphreys's words to be true concerning John Booker, whom at that time I found but moderately versed in astrology; nor could he take the circles of position of the planets, until in that year I instructed him. After my *Introduction* in 1647 became publick, he amended beyond measure, by study partly, and partly upon emulation to keep up his fame and reputation; so that since 1647, I have seen some nativities by him very judiciously performed. When the printer presented him with an *Introduction* of mine, as

---

123 Booker had sole discretion in censorship of all published almanacs during his post as licenser – a power he exercised liberally when intimidated by the precision and insights of Lilly's first *Merlinus Anglicus*. Lilly's note that one could not "distinguish betwixt King and Parliament" – two sides already engaged in hot contention – is particularly telling of the extent of Booker's revisions.

124 Sometimes spelled Dagan, a Mesopotamian god. Here Lilly simply means to say that he received the support of the Presbyterian printer, and five of his connections in the ministry, to freely publish a second edition of his *Merlinus*, so long as he refrained from criticisms on the Presbytery.

soon as they were forth of the press; 'I wish', saith he, 'there was never another but this in England, conditionally I gave one hundred pounds for this'. After that time we were very great friends to his dying day.

In June, 1644, I published *Supernatural Sight*[125]; and, indeed, if I could have procured the dull stationer to have been at charges to have cut the *icon* or form of that prodigious apparition, as I had drawn it forth, it would have given great satisfaction;[126] however, the astrological judgment thereupon had its full event in every particular.

That year also I published the *White King's Prophecy*, of which there were sold in three days eighteen hun-

---

125 Full title, *Supernatural Sights and Apparitions seen in London, June 20th, 1644*. The apparition discussed and interpreted was a series of lightning strikes extended from east to west, flashing in rapid succession, and between flashes a

> yellowish apparition of somewhat in form and shape almost like to a Serpent, incurvating a little each end [...] it seemed to be solid and firm, for I saw no dissipation or dispersion of parts at any time, it ever showed itself of an equal length, neither greater nor smaller, nor did it move from the place where first I beheld it more or less for one hour together. (4–5)

Lilly's judgment on the significance of this apparition is fascinating and provides insight into the varying ways seventeenth-century astrologers interpreted and judged the meaning of natural phenomenon occurring in the sky (mock suns or perihelia, comets, or strange sky apparitions such as the ones described in *Supernatural Sights*).

126 A stationer was responsible for preparing images for print publications, using woodcuts or other natural materials. Lilly was apparently dissatisfied with the "dull stationer" and his rendition of Lilly's illustration.

CHARLES THE FIRST

From a Picture by Vandyck

dred,[127] so that it was oft reprinted: I then made no commentary upon it.

In that year I printed the *Prophetical Merlin*, and had eight pounds for the copy.

I had then no farther intention to trouble the press any more, but Sir Richard Napper having received one of Captain Wharton's *Almanacks* for 1645, under the name Naworth,[128] he came unto me: 'Now, Lilly, you are met withal, see here what Naworth writes'. The words were, he called me 'an impudent senseless fellow, and by name William Lilly'.

Before that time, I was more Cavalier than Roundhead, and so taken notice of; but after that I engaged body and soul in the cause of Parliament, but still with much affection to his Majesty's person and unto monarchy, which I ever loved and approved beyond any government whatsoever; and you will find in this story many passages of civility which I did, and endeavoured to do, with the hazard of my life, for his Majesty: but God had ordered all his affairs and counsels to have no successes; as in the sequel will appear.

To vindicate my reputation, and to cry quittance with Naworth, against whom I was highly incensed, to work

---

127 Even in the height of almanac distribution, a sell-through rate this aggressive was very rare, and an early indication of the prominence Lilly would soon reach as England's leading astrologer.

128 Naworth was the name George Wharton published under, an anagram of his last name. It became a bit of a joke to his detractors who subjected the pseudonym to word-play implying that his commentary was of "no worth."

I went again for *Anglicus*, 1645;[129] which as soon as finished I got to the press, thinking every day one month till it was publick: I therein made use of the King's nativity, and finding that his ascendant was approaching to the quadrature of Mars, about June, 1645, I gave this unlucky judgment; 'If now we fight, a victory stealeth upon us'; and so it did in June, 1645, at Naseby, the most fatal overthrow he ever had.[130]

In this year, 1645, I published a treatise called the *Starry Messenger*, with an interpretation of three suns seen in London, 29th May, 1644, being Charles the Second's birthday: in that book I also put forth an astrological judgment concerning the effects of a solar eclipse, visible the 11th of August, 1645. Two days before its publishing, my antagonist, Captain Wharton, having given his astronomical judgment upon his Majesty's present march from Oxford; therein again fell foul against me and John Booker: Sir Samuel Luke, Governor of Newportpagnel, had the thing came to his garrison from Oxford, which presently was presented unto my view. I had but twelve hours, or thereabout, to answer it, which I did with such success as is incredible; and the printer printed both the *March* and my answer unto it, and produced it to sight, with my *Starry Messenger*,[131] which came forth and was

---

129 The 1645 *Merlinus* contained "a modest reply to M. Wharton, and the Prognostication of his present Almanak printed at Oxford, for 1645."

130 The Battle of Naseby was the first decisive battle of the English Civil War. Led by Sir Thomas Fairfax and Oliver Cromwell, the New Model Army decimated the King's forces.

131 Lilly's witty response was written as a four-page postscript at the end

made publick the very day of the Parliament's great victory obtained against his Majesty in person at Naseby, under the conduct of the Lord Thomas Fairfax.

That book no sooner appeared, but within fourteen days complaint was made to the committee of examinations, Miles Corbet then being Chairman, my mortal enemy, he who after was hanged, drawn, and quartered, for being one of the King's Judges; he grants his warrant, and a messenger to the Serjeant at Arms seizeth my person. As I was going to Westminster with the messenger, I met Sir Philip Stapleton, Sir Christopher Wray, Mr. Denzil Hollis, Mr. Robert Reynolds,[132] who, by great fortune, had the *Starry Messenger* sheet by sheet from me as it came from the press. They presently fell a smiling at me; 'Miles Corbet, Lilly, will punish thee soundly; but fear nothing, we will dine, and make haste to be at the committee time enough to do the business'; and so they most honourably performed; for they, as soon as they came, sat down, and put Mr. Reynolds purposely into the chair, and I was called in; but Corbet being not there, they bid me withdraw until he came; which when he did, I was commanded to appear, and Corbet desired to give the cause of my being in restraint, and of the committee's order. Mr. Reynolds was purposely put into the chair, and continued till my business was over.

Corbet produced my *Anglicus* of 1645, and said there

---

of his *Starry Messenger*.

132 English political leaders who supported the cause of Parliament, each enduring some varying level of injustice throughout their career at the hands of the English crown.

were many scandalous passages therein againſt the Commissioners of Excise in London.[133] He produced one passage, which being openly read by himself, the whole committee adjudged it to signify the errors of sub-officers, but had no relation to the Commissioners themselves, which I affirmatively maintained to be the true meaning as the committee declared.

Then Corbet found out another dangerous place, as he thought, and the words were thus in the printed book – 'In the name of the Father, Son, and Holy Ghoſt, will not the Excise pay the soldiers?'

Corbet very ignorantly read, 'will not the Eclipse pay soldiers?' at which the Committee fell heartily to laugh at him, and so he became silent.

There was a great many Parliament men there; the chamber was full. 'Have you any more againſt Mr. Lilly?' cried the chairman.

'Yes', saith the Sollicitor[134] for the Excise, 'since his *Starry Messenger* came forth we had our house burnt, and the Commissioners pulled by their cloaks in the Exchange'.[135] 'Pray, sir, when was this', asked old Sir Robert Pye, 'that the house was burnt, and the Aldermen abused?' 'It was in such a week', saith he. 'Mr. Lilly, when came the book forth?' 'The very day of Naseby

---

133 This passage was a harsh criticism of the Commission's failure to pay the soldiers their wages for duties already performed. At this point the troops had been many months without pay.

134 Lawyer, or legal advisor.

135 An accusation that Lilly's almanac incited soldiers to riot against the Commissioners and demand their pay.

fight', answered Mr. Reynolds, 'nor needs he be ashamed of writing it: I had it daily as it came forth of the press: it was then found the house to be burnt, and the Aldermen abused, twelve days before the *Starry Messenger* came forth'. 'What a lying fellow art thou', saith Sir Robert Pye, 'to abuse us so!' This he spoke to the Sollicitor. Then stood up one Bassell, a merchant: he inveighed bitterly against me, being a Presbyterian,[136] and would have had my books burnt. 'You smell more of a citizen than a scholar', replied Mr. Francis Drake. I was ordered to withdraw, and by and by was called in, and acquainted the committee did discharge me. But I cried with a loud voice, 'I was under a messenger'; whereupon the committee ordered him or the Serjeant at Arms not to take any fees; Mr. Reynolds saying, 'Literate men never pay any fees'.

But within one week after, I was likely to have had worse success, but that the before-named gentlemen stoutly befriended me. In my Epistle of the *Starry Messenger*, I had been a little too plain with the committee of Leicestershire;[137] who thereof made complaint unto

---

136 The Presbyterians were vehemently opposed to judicial astrology and prophesying by the stars.

137 Lilly's critique of the Roundhead leaders of Leicestershire features accusations of poor administrative decisions, the loss of a stronghold that took years to build, a decreasing morale amongst the soldiers, and the wasting of raised funds:

> Unworthy men have wearied my Pen, disheartened the Gentry to our inevitable loss, and impoverishment of the poor Commonalty, and destruction of those towns so unlucky committed to their charge: Let the

Sir Arthur Hazelrigg, Knight for that county; he was a furious person, and made a motion in the House of Commons against me, and the business was committed to that committee, whereof Baron Rigby was chairman. A day was assigned to hear the matter; in the morning whereof, as I passed by Mr. Pullen's shop in St. Paul's Church-yard,[138] Pullen bad 'God be with you', and named me by name. Mr. Selden being there, and hearing my name, gave direction to call me unto him, where he acquaints me with Hazelrigg's humour[139] and malice towards me, called for the *Starry Messenger*, and having read over the words mentioning that committee, he asked me how I would answer them? I related what I would have said, but he contradicted me, and acquainted me what to say, and how to answer. In the afternoon I went to appear, but there was no committee set, or would sit; for both Mr. Reynolds and Sir Philip Stapleton, and my other friends, had fully acquainted Baron Rigby with the business, and desired him not to

> town of Leicester be hereof an unlucky precedent, which hath been these three years fortifying, and now on the sudden transmitted to his Majesty's forces. What became of the vast sums of money there raised? Why the valiant Gentlemen displaced? And men of inferior rank exalted? Who gives any reason? Unless it was purposely done to betray the town to our enemies, or by loss of that to long the wars another year. You shall see if his Majesty's Providence fortify not that town in less months than we in years; It must be discovered who, or whom have played the plain knaves with us, or else we shall never be at quiet (*Starry Messenger*, A5–A6).

138 St. Paul's Cathedral.
139 Medieval use of the word "humour" means disposition.

call upon me until they appeared; for the matter and charge intended against me was very frivolous, and only presented by a cholerick person[140] to please a company of clowns, meaning the committee of Leicester. Baron Rigby said, if it were so he would not meddle with the matter, but exceedingly desired to see me. Not long after he met Sir Arthur, and acquainting him what friends appeared for me, said, 'I will then prosecute him no further'.

All the ancient astrologers of England were much startled and confounded at my manner of writing, especially old Mr. William Hodges, who lived near Wolverhampton in Staffordshire, and many others who understood astrology competently well, as they thought. Hodges swore I did more by astrology than he could by the crystal, and use thereof, which indeed he understood as perfectly as any one in England. He was a great royalist, but could never hit any thing right for that party, though he much desired it: he resolved questions astrologically; nativities he meddled not with; in things of other nature, which required more curiosity, he repaired to the crystal: his angels were Raphael, Gabriel, and Uriel:[141] his life answered not in holiness and sanctity to what it should, having to deal with those holy angels. Being contemporary with me, I shall relate what my partner John Scott, the same Scott as is before-men-

---

140 Someone quick to anger, of a choleric humor.
141 Archangels in the Judeo-Christian tradition, highly revered, and sometimes called upon in occult practice.

tioned,[142] affirmed of him. John Scott was a little skilful in surgery and physick, so was Will Hodges, and had formerly been a school-master. Scott having some occasions into Staffordshire, addressed himself for a month or six weeks to Hodges, assisted him to dress his patients, let blood, &c. Being to return to London, he desired Hodges to shew him the person and feature of the woman he should marry. Hodges carries him into a field not far from his house, pulls out his crystal, bids Scott set his foot to his, and, after a while, wishes him to inspect the crystal, and observe what he saw there. 'I see', saith Scott, 'a ruddy complexioned wench in a red waistcoat, drawing a can of beer'. 'She must be your wife', said Hodges. 'You are mistaken, Sir', said Scott. 'I am, so soon as I come to London, to marry a tall gentlewoman in the Old Bailey'. 'You must marry the red waistcoat', said Hodges. Scott leaves the country, comes up to London, finds his gentlewoman married: two years after going into Dover, in his return, he refreshed himself at an inn in Canterbury, and as he came into the hall, or first room thereof, he mistook the room, and went into the buttery, where he espied a maid, described by Hodges, as before said, drawing a can of beer, &c. He then more narrowly viewing her person and habit, found her, in all parts, to be the same Hodges had described; after which he became a suitor unto her, and was married unto her; which woman I have often seen. This Scott related unto

---

142 The same Scott that Lilly says used the Mosaical rods in the cloisters of Westminster Abbey in an unsuccessful attempt to find hidden treasure.

me several times, being a very honest person, and made great conscience of what he spoke. Another story of him is as followeth, which I had related from a person which well knew the truth of it.

A neighbour gentleman of Hodges lost his horse; who having Hodges's advice for recovery of him,[143] did again obtain him. Some years after, in a frolick, he thought to abuse him, acquainting a neighbour therewith, viz., that he had formerly lost a horse, went to Hodges, recovered him again, but saith it was by chance; I might have had him without going unto him: 'Come, let's go, I will now put a trick upon him; I will leave some boy or other at the town's-end with my horse, and then go to Hodges and enquire for him'. He did so, gave his horse to a youth, with orders to walk him till he returned. Away he goes with his friend, salutes Mr. Hodges, thanks him for his former courtesy, and now desires the like, having lost a horse very lately. Hodges, after some time of pausing, said; 'Sir, your horse is lost, and never to be recovered'. 'I thought what skill you had', replies the gallant, 'my horse is walking in a lane at the town's-end'. With that Hodges swore (as he was too much given unto that vice) 'your horse is gone, and you will never have him again'. The gentleman departed in great derision of Hodges, and went where he left his horse: when he came there, he found the boy fast asleep upon the ground, the horse gone, the boy's arm in the bridle.

He returns again to Hodges, desiring his aid, being sorry for his former abuse. Old Will swore like a

---

143 That is, recovery of the missing horse.

devil, 'be gone, be gone; go look for your horse'. This business ended not so; for the malicious man brought Hodges into the star-chamber, bound him over to the assizes, put Hodges to great expences: but, by means of the Lord Dudley, if I remember aright, or some other person thereabouts, he overcame the gentleman, and was acquitted.

Besides this, a gentlewoman of my acquaintance, and of credit, in Leicestershire, having lost a pillion-cloth, a very new one, went to desire his judgment. He ordered her such a day to attend at Mountsorrel in Leicestershire, and about twelve o'clock she should see her pillion-cloth upon a horse, and a woman upon it. My friend attended the hour and place; it being told, she must needs warm herself well, and then enquired if any passengers had lately gone by the inn? Unto whom answer was made, there passed by whilst she was at the fire, about half an hour before, a man, and a woman behind him, on horseback. Inquiring of what colour the pillion-cloth was of; it was answered, directly of the colour my friend's was: they pursued, but too late.

In those times, there lived one William Marsh in Dunstable, a man of godly life and upright conversation, a Recusant.[144] By astrology he resolved thievish questions with great success; that was his utmost sole practice. He was many times in trouble; but by Dr. Napper's interest with the Earl of Bolingbroke, Lord Wentworth,

---

144 Someone who refuses to defer to authority, or to comply with a particular statute or regulation.

after Earl of Cleveland, he still continued his practice, the said Earl not permitting any Justice of Peace to vex him.

This man had only two books, *Guido*[145] and *Haly* bound together; he had so mumbled and tumbled the leaves of both, that half one side of every leaf was torn even to the middle. I was familiar with him for many years: he died about 1647.

A word or two of Dr. Napper, who lived at Great Lindford in Buckinghamshire, was parson, and had the advowson[146] thereof. He descended of worshipful parents, and this you must believe; for when Dr. Napper's brother, Sir Robert Napper, a Turkey merchant, was to be made a Baronet in King James's reign, there was some dispute whether he could prove himself a gentleman for three or more descents. 'By my saul', saith King James, 'I will certify for Napper, that he is of above three hundred years standing in his family, all of them, by my saul, gentlemen', &c. However, their family came into England in King Henry the Eighth's time. The parson was Master of Arts; but whether doctorated by degree or courtesy, because of his profession, I know not. Miscarrying one day in the pulpit, he never after used it, but all his life-time kept in his house some excellent scholar or other to officiate for him, with allowance of a good salary: he out-went Forman in physick and holiness of

---

145 Guido Bonatti's thirteenth-century text *Liber Astronomiæ*, or *Book of Astronomy*.

146 The right of a patron to approach to a diocesan bishop a nominee for appointment to a vacant ecclesiastical office or benefice.

life; cured the falling-sickness perfectly by constellated rings,[147] some diseases by amulets, &c.

A maid was much afflicted with the falling sickness,[148] whose parents applied themselves unto him for cure: he framed her a constellated ring, upon wearing whereof, she recovered perfectly. Her parents acquainted some scrupulous divines with the cure of their daughter: 'The cure is done by inchantment', say they. 'Cast away the ring, it's diabolical; God cannot bless you, if you do not cast the ring away'. The ring was cast into the well, whereupon the maid became epileptical as formerly, and endured much misery for a long time. At last her parents cleansed the well, and recovered the ring again; the maid wore it, and her fits took her no more. In this condition she was one year or two; which the Puritan ministers there adjoining hearing, never left off, till they procured her parents to cast the ring quite away; which done, the fits returned in such violence, that they were enforced to apply to the Doctor again, relating at large the whole story, humbly imploring his once more assistance; but he could not be procured to do any thing, only said, those who despised God's mercies, were not capable or worthy of enjoying them.

I was with him in 1632, or 1633, upon occasion. He had me up into his library, being excellently furnished with very choice books: there he prayed almost one hour; he invocated several angels in his prayer,

---

147 A group or cluster of rings endowed with magical properties.
148 Epilepsy.

viz.* Michael, Gabriel, Raphael, Uriel, &c. We parted.

He instructed many ministers in astrology, would lend them whole cloak-bags of books; protected them from harm and violence, by means of his power with the Earl of Bolingbroke.† He would confess my master Evans knew more than himself in some things: and some time before he died, he got his cousin Sir Richard to set a figure to see when he should die. Being brought him; 'Well', he said, 'the old man will live this winter, but in the spring he will die; welcome Lord Jesus, thy will be done'. He had many enemies: Cotta, Doctor of physick in Northampton, wrote a sharp book of witchcraft, wherein, obliquely, he bitterly inveighed against the Doctor.

In 1646, I printed a collection of Prophecies, with the explanation and verification of Aquila, or the *White King's Prophecy*;[149] as also the nativities of Bishop Laud and Thomas Earl of Strafford, and a most learned speech by him intended to have been spoke upon the scaffold. In this year 1646, after a great consideration,

* The collect read on Michaelmas-day, seems to allow of praying to angels. At some times, upon great occasions, he had conference with Michael, but very rarely.
† Lord Wentworth, after Earl of Cleveland.

---

149 A prophecy from the seventh century, so called for the contents of its second stanza: "Moreover, it shall be reported, and pointed, as it were, with the finger, yonder is the White and Noble King." The full text of this prophecy is translated from the Latin and interpreted by Lilly in his *The Prophecy of the White King*, 23–32.

and many importunities, I began to fix upon thoughts of an *Introduction unto Astrology*, which was very much wanting, and as earnestly longed for by many persons of quality. Something also much occasioned and hastened the impression, viz. the malevolent barking of Presbyterian ministers in their weekly sermons, reviling the professors thereof, and myself particularly by name.

Secondly, I thought it a duty incumbent upon me, to satisfy the whole kingdom of the lawfulness thereof, by framing a plain and easy method for any person but of indifferent capacity to learn the art, and instruct himself therein, without any other master than my *Introduction*; by which means, when many understood it, I should have more partners and assistants to contradict all and every antagonist.

Thirdly, I found it best as unto point of time, because many of the soldiers were wholly for it, and many of the Independant party; and I had abundance of worthy men in the House of Commons, my assured friends, no lovers of Presbytery, which then were in great esteem, and able to protect the art; for should the Presbyterian party have prevailed, as they thought of nothing less than to be Lords of all, I knew well they would have silenced my pen annually, and committed the *Introduction* unto everlasting silence.

Fourthly, I had something of conscience touched my spirit, and much elevated my conceptions, believing God had not bestowed those abilities upon me, to bury them under a bushel; for though my education was very mean, yet, by my continual industry, and God's great mercy, I found myself capable to go forward with the work, and to commit the issue thereof unto Divine Providence.

I had a hard task in hand to begin the first part hereof, and much labour I underwent to methodize it as it is.

I ingenuously confess unto you (Arts' great Mecænas,[150] noble Esquire Ashmole,) no mortal man had any share in the composition or ordering of the first part thereof, but my only self. You are a person of great reading, yet I well know you never found the least trace thereof in any author yet extant.[151]

In composing, contriving, ordering, and framing thereof (viz. the first part) a great part of that year was spent. I again perused all, or most, authors I had, sometimes adding, at other times diminishing, until at last I thought it worthy of the press. When I came to frame the second part thereof, having formerly collected out of many manuscripts, and exchanged rules with the most able professors I had acquaintance with, in transcribing those papers for impression, I found, upon a strict in-

---

150 Gaius Mæcenas was a first-century BCE friend and advisor to the first emperor of Rome, Cæsar Augustus. He was a great patron of the arts, and his last name is often used to indicate someone who is a patron, defender or champion of the arts.

151 Lilly's *Christian Astrology* contains three books – the first, an introduction to the basics of astrology (symbols, calculations, how to rectify a figure, definitions of planetary conditions, a list of the things signified by the planets and signs, etc.); the second, an introduction to horary astrology; and the third, an introduction to natal astrology. While Lilly often references (sometimes copied verbatim) the writings of historical astrologers, particularly Haly, Sahl, and Bonatti, here he makes clear that his first book was wholly his own work.

quisition, those rules were, for the most part, defective; so that once more I had now a difficult labour to correct their deficiency, to new rectify them according to art; and lastly, considering the multiplicity of daily questions propounded unto me, it was as hard a labour as might be to transcribe the papers themselves with my own hand. The desire I had to benefit posterity and my country, at last overcame all difficulties; so that what I could not do in one year, I perfected early the next year, 1647; and then in that year, viz. 1647, I finished the third book of* nativities,† during the composing whereof, for seven whole weeks, I was shut up of the plague, burying in that time two maid-servants thereof; yet towards November that year, the Introduction, called by the name of *Christian Astrology*, was made publick. There being, in those times, some smart difference between the army and the Parliament, the head-quarters of the army were at Windsor, whither I was carried with a coach and four horses,[152] and John Booker with me. We were welcome thither,

* The name of the person whose nativity is directed and judged, is Mr. Thompson, whose father had been some time an inn-keeper at the White-Hart in Newark.
† I devised the forms and fashions of the several schemes. E.A.

---

152 Lilly and Booker were called to Windsor by General Fairfax. Traveling by coach was a precaution against the rising political tensions that resulted in violent outbreaks, at that time growing more frequent in the streets of London.

and feasted in a garden where General Fairfax lodged. We were brought to the General, who bid us kindly welcome to Windsor; and, in effect, said thus much:

'That God had blessed the army with many signal victories, and yet their work was not finished. He hoped God would go along with them until his work was done. They sought not themselves, but the welfare and tranquillity of the good people, and whole nation; and, for that end, were resolved to sacrifice both their lives and their own fortunes. As for the art we studied, he hoped it was lawful and agreeable to God's word: he understood it not; but doubted not but we both feared God; and therefore had a good opinion of us both'. Unto his speech I presently made this reply:

'My Lord, I am glad to see you here at this time.

'Certainly, both the people of God, and all others of this nation, are very sensible of God's mercy, love, and favour unto them, in directing the Parliament to nominate and elect you General of their armies, a person so religious, so valiant.

'The several unexpected victories obtained under your Excellency's conduct, will eternize the same unto all posterity.

'We are confident of God's going along with you and your army, until the great work for which he ordained you both, is fully perfected; which we hope will be the conquering and subversion of your's and the Parliament's enemies, and then a quiet settlement and firm peace over all the nation, unto God's glory, and full satisfaction of tender consciences.

'Sir, as for ourselves, we trust in God; and, as Christians, believe in him. We do not study any art but what is lawful, and consonant to the scriptures, fathers, and antiquity; which we humbly desire you to believe', &c.

This ended, we departed, and went to visit Mr. Peters[153] the minister, who lodged in the castle, whom we found reading an idle pamphlet come from London that morning. 'Lilly, thou art herein', says he. 'Are not you there also?' I replied. 'Yes, that I am', quoth he. – The words concerning me were these:

> From th' oracles of the Sibyls so silly,
> The curst predictions of William Lilly,
> And Dr. Sybbald's Shoe-lane Philly,
>   Good Lord, deliver me.

After much conference with Hugh Peters, and some private discourse betwixt us two, not to be divulged, we parted, and so came back to London.

King Charles the First, in the year 1646, April 27, went unto the Scots, then in this nation. Many desired my judgment, in time of his absence, to discover the way he might be taken: which I would never be drawn unto, or give any direction concerning his person.

There were many lewd Mercuries[154] printed both in

---

153 Hugh Peters, Independent minister and supporter of the Parliamentary cause.

154 Pamphlets, newsletters or newspapers, generally rallied to some cause (e.g., the *Mercurius Britannicus* was a Parliamentary paper, the *Mercurius Pragmaticus* a Royalist one).

London and Oxford, wherein I was sufficiently abused, in this year, 1646. I had then my ascendant *ad* ♊ ☌, and ☽ *ad propriun*.[155] The Presbyterians were, in their pulpits, as merciless as the Cavaliers in their pamphlets.

About this time, the most famous mathematician of all Europe,* Mr. William Oughtred, parson of Aldbury in Surry, was in danger of sequestration by the Committee of or for plundered ministers; (*Ambo-dexters*[156] they were;) several inconsiderable articles were deposed and sworn against him, material enough to have sequestered him, but that, upon his day of hearing, I applied myself to Sir Bolstrode Whitlock, and all my own old friends, who in such numbers appeared in his behalf, that though the chairman and many other Presbyterian members were stiff against him, yet he was cleared by the major number. The truth is, he had a considerable parsonage, and that only was enough to sequester

> * This gentleman I was very well acquainted with, having lived at the house over-against his, at Aldbury in Surrey, three or four years. E.A.

---

155 Roughly, "To their respective places." This is another piece of evidence that Lilly used and directed a chart with his natal Moon in Pisces, as both ascendant and Moon would have been directed by primary motion into Gemini by 1646. If his Moon had been in Capricorn, as James Blackwell and Gadbury argue, his Moon would have been directed to Taurus in 1646, which would directly contradict Lilly's passage here.

156 A literal meaning is to be able to play with either hand, an illustration of the Committee's tendency to sometimes serve parsons, sometimes abuse them.

HUGH PETERS

From an Original Picture

any moderate judgment: he was also well known to affect his Majesty. In these times many worthy ministers lost their livings or benefices, for not complying with the *Three-penny Directory*.[157] Had you seen (O noble Esquire) what pitiful ideots were prefered into sequestrated church-benefices, you would have been grieved in your soul; but when they came before the classis of divines, could those simpletons but only say, they were converted by hearing such a sermon, such a lecture, of that godly man Hugh Peters, Stephen Marshall, or any of that gang, he was presently admitted.[158]

In 1647, I published the *World's Catastrophe*, the *Prophecies of Ambrose Merlin*, with the *Key* wherewith to unlock those obstruse Prophecies; also *Trithemius of the*

---

157 Full title, *The Directory of Public Worship*, first introduced when Parliament abolished the *Book of Common Prayer* in 1645. *The Book of Common Prayer* was an integral part of monarchic Anglican liturgy, used to enforce religious uniformity across the kingdom. King Charles I sought to prosecute those who adopted the *Directory* as this was seen as a direct challenge of Charles I's divine right to rule. The *Directory* enjoyed a very short lifespan, disappearing altogether by 1662, largely due to Parliament's failure to successfully establish an English Presbyterian church. Lilly's casual reference to it as the T*hree-penny Directory* was to underscore his low opinion of the Presbytery and their trifling work of propaganda, not worth more than three pence.

158 Once a parsonage had been sequestered or confiscated by the state for not having adopted the Directory, hard-working ministers could be replaced by seemingly anyone who knew the right names to drop and sympathies to express.

Government of the World by the presiding Angels;[159] these came forth all in one book.[160]

The two first were exquisitely translated by yourself, (most learned Sir) as I do ingenuously acknowledge in my *Epistle unto the Reader*,[161] with a true character of the worth and admirable parts, unto which I refer any that do desire to read you perfectly delineated. I was once resolved to have continued *Trithemius* for some succeeding years, but multiplicity of employment impeded me. The study required, in that kind of learning, must be sedentary, of great reading, sound judgment, which no man can accomplish except he wholly retire, use prayer, and

---

159 Johannes Trithemius, a German Benedictine and occultist who taught such minds as Agrippa and Paracelsus, wrote "Government of the World by the Presiding Angels" as a treastise in mundane astrology. Lilly duplicates some of Trithemius's source material here in his 1647 *World's Catastrophe*.

160 *World's Catastrophe* contained a number of calculated predictions for Europe until the year 1666, including an exposition on mock suns seen in England on 3 April 1647. It also included *A Whip for Wharton*, a defense of Lilly against Wharton's most recent critiques.

161 Elias Ashmole and Lilly were in the early stages of their relationship at the release of *World's Catastrophe*, having only been introduced the year before. For his considerable contributions to the pamphlet, Lilly recognized and praised the young Ashmole in its opening:

In astrologie he is well versed, and in Antiquities no mean student; for who shall read Merlin in the Latin copy, shall wonder at the dexterity and sharp apprehension of this gentleman, that being in years so young should understand and distinguish terms and names, so obsolete, and no infrequently vulgar; and yet hath rendered them in our mother-tongue in so compliant and decent Phrase, as might have become an Antiquary of double his years. (*World's Catastrophe*, A2)

accompany himself with angelical consorts.[162]

His Majesty Charles the First, having entrusted the Scots with his person,[163] was, for money, delivered into the hands of the English Parliament, and, by several removals, was had to Hampton-Court,[164] about July or August 1647; for he was there, and at that time when my house was visited with the plague. He was desirous to escape from the soldiery, and to obscure himself for some time near London, the citizens whereof began now to be unruly, and alienated in affection from the Parliament, inclining wholly to his Majesty, and very averse to the army.[165] His Majesty was well informed of all this, and thought to make good use hereof; besides, the army and Parliament were at some odds, who should be masters. Upon the King's intention to escape, and with his consent, Madam Whorewood[166] (whom you knew very well, worthy Esquire) came to receive my judgment, viz.

---

162 It was a commonly held medieval belief that a respectful consorting with angels could impart wisdom and understanding incapable of achievement by personal study alone.

163 After a series of hardships and epic defeats (beginning with the Battle of Naseby in June 1645), Charles I repaired to the Scots for shelter and a time to regain strength and stabilize. The first of three civil wars (collectively, the "English Civil War") ended when the Scots handed Charles I over to the English Parliament and he was imprisoned.

164 Hampton Court Palace was to become Charles I's palace and his prison.

165 The divide between soldiers and Parliament came for a number of reasons, not least of which was Parliament's lack of urgency in paying the soldiers their earned wages.

166 Jane Whorwood, a fervent Royalist activist during the English Civil War.

In what quarter of this nation he might be moſt safe, and not to be discovered until himself pleased.

When she came to my door, I told her I would not let her come into my house for I buried a maid-servant of the plague very lately. 'I fear not the plague, but the pox',[167] quoth she; so up we went. After erection of my figure, I told her about twenty miles (or thereabouts) from London, and in Essex, I was certain he might continue undiscovered. She liked my judgment very well; and, being herself of a sharp judgment, remembered a place in Essex about that diſtance, where was an excellent house, and all conveniences for his reception. Away she went, early next morning, unto Hampton-Court, to acquaint his Majeſty; but see the misfortune: He, either guided by his own approaching hard fate, or misguided by *Ashburnham,[168] went away in the night-time weſtward, and surrendered himself to

* This Ashburnham was turned out of the House of Commons the 3d of November, 1667, for taking a bribe of five hundred pounds of the merchants. I was informed hereof 26th November, 1667.

---

167 Whorwood had smallpox when she was a little girl.
168 John Ashburnham was friend and confidant to the King, and as a believer in astrology may have been the one to suggest Whorwood approach Lilly for guidance.

Hammond,[169] in the Isle of Wight.

Whilst his Majesty was at Hampton-Court Alderman Adams sent his Majesty one thousand pounds in gold, five hundred whereof he gave Madam Whorewood. I believe I had twenty pieces of that very gold for my share.

I have something more to write of Charles the First's misfortunes, wherein I was concerned; the matter happened in 1648, but I thought good to insert it here, having after this no more occasion to mention him.

His Majesty being in Carisbrook-Castle in the Isle

---

169 Robert Hammond, officer in the New Model Army under Oliver Cromwell and nephew of Royalist churchman Henry Hammond. Robert Hammond was introduced to King Charles I by his uncle some time earlier. He gave the King salutes of royalty and fealty, to the extent that Charles I believed him to be in the pocket of the monarchic cause. Sir John Berkeley informed Hammond in 1647 that the King had escaped Hampton Court and intended to flee to the Isle of Wight and place himself under Hammond's protection, and this placed great unrest in Hammond's heart.

Shortly before Charles I came to the Isle of Wight to seek refuge from his attackers, the New Model Army was operating independently from Parliament, and as Lilly says earlier, "inclining wholly to his Majesty." What Hammond knew that the King did not was that the New Model Army had no intentions of keeping its promises to the King. Internally conflicted by his Army's dishonesty, and having no desire to participate in the deceit, Hammond wrote to the Parliament to advise the MPs of the sticky situation. Hammond quickly received instructions from Parliament to keep Charles I on the island, and set a constant watch over him. Parliament also instructed that Ashburnham, Berkeley and William Legge (a Royalist army officer also on the Isle of Wight) be taken as prisoners, commands that Hammond reluctantly obeyed. Despite his early relationship with the King, Hammond found that he gradually became his jailer and warden.

of Wight, the Kentish men, in great numbers, rose in arms, and joined with the Lord Goring;[170] a considerable number of the best ships revolted from the Parliament; the citizens of London were forward to rise against the Parliament; his Majesty laid his design to escape out of prison, by sawing the iron bars of his chamber window; a small ship was provided, and anchored not far from the castle to bring him into Sussex; horses were provided ready to carry him through Sussex into Kent, so that he might be at the head of the army in Kent, and from thence to march immediately to London, where thousands then would have armed for him. The Lady Whorewood came to me, acquaints me herewith. I got G. Farmer (who was a most ingenious lock-smith, and dwelt in Bowlane) to make a saw to cut the iron bars in sunder, I mean to saw them, and aqua fortis[171] besides. His Majesty in a small time did his work; the bars gave liberty for him to go out; he was out with his body till he came to his breast; but then his heart failing, he proceeded no farther:[172] when this was discovered, as soon after it was, he was narrowly looked after, and no opportunity after that could be devised to enlarge him. About

---

170 George Goring, the first Earl of Norwich, Royalist supporter and politician, who led the Kents in their rebellion against Parliament.

171 "Strong water," meaning nitric acid.

172 Charles I may have had reservations about following plans either designed by or involving Lilly, as his almanacs and pamphlets had up to this point shown him to be a clear Parliamentary supporter (despite Lilly's harsh critiques of the then Parliament's inability or unwillingness to stabilize the nation).

September the Parliament sent their Commissioners with propositions[173] unto him into the Isle of Wight, the Lord William Sea being one; the Lady Whorewood comes again unto me from him or by his consent, to be directed: After perusal of my figure, I told her the Commissioners would be there such a day; I elected a day and hour when to receive the Commissioners and propositions; and as soon as the propositions were read, to sign them, and make haste with all speed to come up with the Commissioners to London. The army being then far distant from London, and the city enraged stoutly against them, he promised he would do so. That night the Commissioners came, and old Sea and his Majesty had private conference till one in the morning: the King acquaints Sea with his intention, who clearly dissuaded him from signing the propositions, telling him they were not fit for him to sign; that he had many friends in the House of Lords, and some in the House of Commons; that he would procure more, and then they would frame more easy propositions. This flattery of this unfortunate Lord occasioned his Majesty to wave the advice I and some others that wished his prosperity had given, in expectation of that which afterwards could never be gained. The army having some notice hereof from one of the Commissioners, who had an eye upon old Sea, hasted unto London, and made the citizens very quiet; and besides, the Parliament and army kept a bet-

---

173 Conditions and terms of the King's release and relinquishing of power.

ter correspondency afterwards with each other.[174]

Whilſt the King was at Windsor-Caſtle, once walking upon the leads there, he looked upon Captain Wharton's *Almanack*: 'My book', saith he, 'speaks well as to the weather':[175] One William Allen ſtanding by; 'what', saith he, 'saith his antagoniſt, Mr. Lilly?' 'I do not care for Lilly', said his Majeſty, 'he hath been always againſt me', and became a little bitter in his expressions. 'Sir', saith Allen, 'the man is an honeſt man, and writes but what his art informs him'. 'I believe it', said his Majeſty, 'and that Lilly underſtands aſtrology as well as any man in Europe'. *Exit Rex Carolus.*[176]

In 1648 I published a *Treatise of the Three Suns*, seen the winter preceding; as also an Aſtrological Judgment upon a Conjunction of Saturn and Mars 28 June, in 11 degrees 8 minutes of Gemini.

I commend unto your perusal that book and the *Prophetical Merlin*, which, seriously considered, (Oh worthy Esquire) will more inſtruct your judgement (*De*

---

174 An Army spy delivered the news of the King's knowledge that the Army was far removed from London, and how that informed his plans to enter the city. The Army then came swiftly to London to minimize the unrest and garrison the town. Parliament took quick note of how their disharmony with the New Model Army had a negative impact on their public reputation, and as Lilly says, made a more deliberate effort thereafter to be in better communication (to what degree of success is debatable).

175 "Weather" to mean the political climate. Royalist Wharton was known to make predictions of fortune and victory for the King's forces, prognostications that history now regards as wishful thinking.

176 "King Charles exits."

generalibus contingentibus Mundi[177]) than all the authors you yet ever met with.

In this year, for very great considerations, the Council of State gave me in money fifty pounds, and a pension of one hundred pounds *per Annum*, which for two years I received, but no more: upon some discontents I after would not or did require it. The cause moving them was this; they could get no intelligence out of France, although they had several agents there for that purpose. I had formerly acquaintance with a secular priest, at this time confessor to one of the Secretaries; unto him I wrote, and by that means had perfect knowledge of the chiefest concernments of France, at which they admired; but I never yet, until this day, revealed the name of the person.

One occasion why I deserted that employment was, because Scott, who had eight hundred pounds *per Annum* for intelligence, would not contribute any occasion to gratify my friend: And another thing was, I received some affront from Gualter Frost their Secretary, one that was a principal minister belonging to the Council of State. Scott was ever my enemy, the other knave died of a gangrene in his arm suddenly after.

In 1648 and 1649, that I might encourage young students in astrology, I publickly read over the first part of my *Introduction*, wherein there are many things contained, not easily to be understood.

And now we are entered into the year 1649: his Maj-

---

[177] "On the general contingencies of the world."

esty being at St. James's House, in January of that year,[178] I begun its observations thus:

"I am serious, I beg and expect justice; either fear or shame begins to question offenders.

"The lofty cedars begin to divine a thundering hurricane is at hand; God elevates men contemptible.

"Our demigods are sensible we begin to dislike their actions very much in London, more in the country.

"Blessed be God, who encourages his servants, makes them valiant, and of undaunted spirits, to go on with his decrees: upon a sudden, great expectations arise, and men generally believe a quiet and calm time draws nigh".

In Christmas holidays, the Lord Gray of Grooby[179] and Hugh Peters sent for me to Somerset-House, with directions to bring them two of my Almanacks. — I did so; Peters and he read January's Observations.

'If we are not fools and knaves', saith he, 'we shall do justice': then they whispered. I understood not their meaning till his Majesty was beheaded. They applied what I wrote of justice, to be understood of his Majesty,

---

178 The year and month of King Charles I's execution.
179 Lord Thomas Gray of Groby, a Parliamentary MP for Leicester who supported the execution of the King. Not directly discussed in Lilly's autobiography was the event that became known as "Pride's Purge." Four days after the New Model Army invaded London (December of 1648), Colonel Pride banned or arrested those members of Parliament that opposed either the New Model Army, or calling the King to stand trial for his wrongdoings. Those that remained became known as the Rump Parliament. Lord Gray was the secret informant who instructed Pride on whom to remove or arrest.

which was contrary to my intention;[180] for Jupiter, the first day of January, became direct; and Libra is a sign signifying Justice; I implored for justice generally upon such as had cheated in their places, being treasurers, and such like officers. I had not then heard the least intimation of bringing the King unto trial, and yet the first day thereof I was casually there, it being upon a Saturday; for going to Westminster every Saturday in the afternoon, in these times, at White-hall I casually met Peters; 'Come, Lilly, wilt thou go hear the King tried?' 'When?' said I. 'Now, just now; go with me'. I did so, and was permitted by the guard of soldiers to pass up to the King's-Bench. Within one quarter of an hour came the Judges, presently his Majesty, who spoke excellently well, and majestically, without impediment in the least when he spoke. I saw the silver top of his staff unexpectedly fall to the ground,

---

180 That Lilly was asked to bring two almanacs may imply that his hosts were, surreptitiously, searching for a suitable astrological election for regicide. Whether or not Lilly was oblivious to his hosts' secret interests, as he says, is open to speculation.

On 19 January 1648 (OS), one day before the trial of King Charles I commenced, Lilly was asked to judge via horary whether or not the King would be beheaded. Lilly judged that the King would be put to death. The querent implored Lilly to look for an "out," a way for the King to escape the fateful end to his trial. Lilly judged that if the King could live past the thirtieth of that month (OS), there were hopes for the King's escape. This information found its way into enemy hands, and though Lilly explains this was not his intent, it may have been a factor in the court's decision to execute the King on 30 January. *See the Introduction for more information on this chart.*

which was took up by Mr. Rushworth:[181] and then I heard Bradshaw the Judge say to his Majesty,

'Sir, instead of answering the court, you interrogate their power, which becomes not one in your condition' –

These words pierced my heart and soul, to hear a subject thus audaciously to reprehend his Sovereign, who ever and anon replied with great magnanimity and prudence.

After that his Majesty was beheaded, the Parliament for some years effected nothing either for the publick peace or tranquillity of the nation, or settling religion as they had formerly promised. The interval of time betwixt his Majesty's death and Oliver Cromwel's displacing them,[182] was wholly consumed in voting for themselves,

181 A salient note by Dawson in his "A Time To Die":

Lilly mentions the well known, but seemingly trivial incident where the silver top of Charles's walking stick falls off when he prodded the prosecutor John Cook in the back as Cook was giving his opening declaration. Charles was used to having things done for him, so as the top of his cane rolled around the hushed courtroom floor he waited expectantly for Cook to retrieve it for him; but Cook ignored him and continued with his opening declaration. This was the moment when Charles realised just how powerless he was, and that this time his opponents meant business. In those few chilling seconds Charles was lost for words as it now dawned on him that, just like the top of his cane, his own head could soon be rolling around the floor. All those present considered this incident an ill omen, including Charles himself. Later historians would embellish the story by stating that Charles was humiliated into having to retrieve the silver top himself; but It would seem that Lilly's offhand comment sounds nearer the truth and that it was the clerk of the court Mr Rushworth that retrieved it and handed it back to Charles.

182 The forcible dismissal of the Rump Parliament, occurring on 20 April

and bringing their own relations to be members of Parliament, thinking to make a trade thereof.

The week, or three or four days before his Majesty's beheading, one Major Sydenham, who had commands in Scotland, came to take his leave of me, and told me the King was to be put to death, which I was not willing to believe, and said, 'I could not be persuaded the Parliament could find any Englishman so barbarous, that would do that foul action'. 'Rather', saith he, 'than they should want such a man, these arms of mine should do it'. He went presently after into Scotland, and upon the first engagement against them, was slain, and his body miserably cut and mangled.

In 1651 I published *Monarchy or no Monarchy*, and in the latter end thereof some hieroglyphics of my own, composed, at spare time, by the occult learning, many of those types having representations of what should from thence succeed in England, and have since had verification.

I had not that learning from books, or any manuscript I ever yet met withal, it is reduced from a cabal lodging in astrology, but so mysterious and difficult to be attained, that I have not yet been acquainted with any who had that knowledge. I will say no more thereof, but that the asterisms and signs and constellations give greatest light thereunto.[183]

1653, and predicted in Lilly's *Merlinus Anglicus* for 1652/3.
183 I.e., the hieroglyphics are coded astrological language, with astrological truths and asterisms deeply embedded, not easily seen, or even then understood, but put down to posterity all the same for those cunning and

During Bradshaw's being President of the Council of State, it was my happiness to procure Captain Wharton his liberty,[184] which when Bradshaw understood, said, 'I will be an enemy to Lilly, if ever he come before me'. Sir Bolstrode Whitlock broke the ice first of all on behalf of Captain Wharton: after him the Committee, unto whom his offence had been committed, spoke for him, and said he might well be bailed or enlarged: I had spoken to the Committee the morning of his delivery, who thereupon were so civil unto him, especially Sir William Ermin of Lincolnshire, who at first wondered I appeared not against him; but upon my humble request, my long continued antagonist was enlarged and had his liberty.

In 1651 I purchased one hundred and ten pounds *per Annum* in fee-farm rents for one thousand and thirty pounds. I paid all in ready money; but when his Majesty King Charles the Second, 1660, was restored,[185] I lost it all again, and it returned to the right owner;[186] the loss thereof never afflicted me, for I have ever reduced my mind according to my fortune. I was drawn in by several

---

learned enough to find out their meanings.

184 Wharton was arrested in 1648 for the excoriating commentary against Parliament in his *No Merlin nor Mercury: but a New Alamack* (1648). At Ashmole's request, Lilly approached Whitelock to advocate for Wharton's release.

185 The Restoration of the monarchy came in 1660 at the coronation of King Charles II, ending the republican period called the Interregnum.

186 The circumstances surrounding this financial loss are unknown. Parker notes in his *Familiar to All*, "It may be that some royalist was able, successfully, to claim that Lilly had come by the properties as a result of Parliamentary confiscation" (203).

persons to make that simple purchase. The year I bought it, I had my ascendant directed into a Trine of Jupiter first,[187] and in the same year into the *Cauda Draconis*[188] – my fortune into a quadrant of Mercury.[189] When Colchester was besieged,[190] John Booker and myself were sent for, where we encouraged the soldiers, assuring them the town would very shortly be surrendered, as indeed it was: I would willingly have obtained leave to enter the town, to have informed Sir Charles Lucas, whom I well knew, with the condition of affairs as they then stood, he being deluded by false intelligence:[191] at that time my scholar Humphreys was therein, who many times deluded the Governor with expectation of relief; but failing very many times with his lies, at last he had the bastinado,[192] was put in prison, and inforced to become a soldier; and well it was he escaped so. – During my being there, the steeple of St. Mary's Church was much battered by two cannons purposely placed: I was

---

187 Lilly's ascendant would need to be in the fourth or fifth degree of Pisces to be directed to a trine to Jupiter in 1651.

188 "Dragon's Tail," the Latinized medieval name for the South Node of the Moon.

189 This may be in reference to Venus, Lilly's second house ruler, which would be directed to the early degrees of Leo by 1651, squaring his natal Mercury at 4° Taurus.

190 Colchester was taken by Lord Goring and his Royalist army in 1648. The ensuing siege by Parliamentary forces took more than eleven weeks before Goring surrendered.

191 Lucas was beheaded after Goring's surrender. Lilly, undoubtedly, wanted to warn him of his dire condition.

192 Whipping of the feet, a form of corporal punishment.

there one day about three of the clock in the afternoon, talking with the cannoneer, when presently he desired us to look to ourselves, for he perceived by his perspective glass there was a piece charged in the castle against his work, and ready to be discharged. I ran for haste under an old ash-tree, and immediately the cannon-bullet came hissing quite over us. 'No danger now', saith the gunner, 'but begone, for there are five more charging', which was true; for two hours after those cannons were discharged, and unluckily killed our cannoneer and matross. I came the next morning and saw the blood of the two poor men lie upon the planks: we were well entertained at the head-quarters, and after two whole days abiding there, came for London.

But we prosecute our story again, and say that in the year 1652 I purchased my house and some lands in Hersham, in the parish of Walton upon Thames, in the county of Surrey, where I now live; intending by the blessing of God, when I found it convenient, to retire into the country, there to end my days in peace and tranquillity; for in London my practice was such, I had none or very little time afforded me to serve God, who had been so gracious unto me. The purchase of the house and lands, and buildings, stood me in nine hundred and fifty pounds sterling, which I have very much augmented.

The Parliament now grows odious unto all good men, the members whereof became insufferable in their pride, covetousness, self-ends, laziness, minding nothing but how to enrich themselves. Much heart-burning now arose betwixt the Presbyterian and Independant,[193] the latter siding with the army, betwixt whose two judgments there was no medium. Now came up, or first appeared, that monstrous people called Ranters:[194] and many other novel opinions, in themselves heretical and scandalous, were countenanced by members of Parliament, many whereof were of the same judgment. Justice was neglected, vice countenanced, and all care of the common good laid aside. Every judgment almost groaned under the heavy burthen they then suffered; the army neglected; the city of London scorned; the ministry, especially those who were orthodox and serious, honest or virtuous, had no countenance; my soul began to loath the very name of a Parliament, or Parliament-men. There yet remained in the House very able, judicious, and worthy patriots; but they, by their silence, only served themselves: all was carried on by a rabble of dunces, who being the greater number, voted what seemed best to their non-intelligent fancies.

In this year I published *Annas Tenebrosus*,[195] which book I did not so entitle, because of the great obscurity of the solar eclipse, by so many prattled of to no purpose, but because of those underhand and clandes-

---

193 These two sides formed the major factions within Parliament. Their disagreements were such that the Parliament was reduced to in-fighting and its members became ineffective at carrying out their posts, to the detriment of the English people.

194 English dissenters, hailed by some as religious libertines and violent radicals by others.

195 More accurately, *Annus Tenebrosus*, or "The Dark Year."

tine counsels held in England by the soldiery, of which I would never, but in generals, give any knowledge unto any Parliament man. I had wrote publickly in 1650, that the Parliament should not continue, but a new government should arise, &c.

In my next year's *Anglicus*, upon rational grounds in astrology, I was so bold as to aver therein, that the Parliament stood upon a tottering foundation, and that the commonalty and soldiery would join together against them.[196]

My *Anglicus*[197] was for a whole week every day in the Parliament House, peeped into by the Presbyterians, one disliking this sentence, another finds another fault, others misliked the whole; so in the end a motion was made, that *Anglicus* should be inspected by the Committee for plundered ministers; which being done, they were to return them to the House, viz. report its errors.

A messenger attached me by a warrant from that Committee; I had private notice ere the messenger came, and hasted unto Mr. Speaker Lenthall, ever my friend. He was exceeding glad to see me, told me what was done; called for Anglicus, marked the passages which tormented the Presbyterians so highly. I presently sent for Mr. Warren the printer, an assured Cavalier, obliterated what was most offensive, put in other more significant words, and desired only to have six

---

196 This prophecy and its highly politicized response is discussed at some length in the introduction to this edition of Lilly's autobiography.
197 *Merlini Anglici Ephemeris* for 1653.

amended against next morning, which very honestly he brought me. I told him my design was to deny the book found fault with, to own only the six books. I told him, I doubted he would be examined. 'Hang them', said he, 'they are all rogues. I'll swear myself to the devil ere they shall have an advantage against you by my oath'.

The day after, I appeared before the Committee, being thirty-six in number that day; whereas it was observed, at other times, it was very difficult to get five of them together. At first they shewed me the true *Anglicus*, and asked if I wrote and printed it. I took the book and inspected it very heedfully; and when I had done so, said thus:

'This is none of my book, some malicious Presbyterian hath wrote it, who are my mortal enemies; I disown it'. The Committee looked upon one another like distracted men, not imagining what I presently did; for I presently pulled out of my pocket six books, and said, 'These I own, the others are counterfeits, published purposely to ruin me'. The Committee were now more vexed than before: not one word was spoke a good while; at last, many of them, or the greatest number of them, were of opinion to imprison me. Some were for Newgate, others for the Gate-House; but then one Brown of Sussex, called the Presbyterian beadle, whom the Company of Stationers had bribed to be my friend, by giving him a new *Book of Martyrs*;[198] he, I say, preached unto the

---

198 Foxe's *Book of Martyrs*, a caustic account of Protestant sufferings and persecutions at the hands of the Roman Catholic Church (and in particular, the Church of England), first published in the sixteenth century.

WILLIAM LENTHALL

*Speaker of the House of Commons
From a Miniature by Cooper*

Committee this doctrine, that neither Newgate or the Gate-House were prisons unto which at any time the Parliament sent their prisoners: it was most convenient for the Serjeant at Arms to take me in custody.

Mr. Strickland,[199] who had for many years been the Parliament's Ambassador or Agent in Holland, when he saw how they inclined, spoke thus:

'I came purposely into the Committee this day to see the man who is so famous in those parts where I have so long continued: I assure you his name is famous all over Europe: I come to do him justice. A book is produced by us, and said to be his; he denies it; we have not proved it, yet will commit him. Truly this is great injustice. It is likely he will write next year, and acquaint the whole world with our injustice; and so well he may. It is my opinion, first to prove the book to be his, ere he be committed'.

Another old friend of mine, Mr. R.[200] spoke thus:

'You do not know the many services this man hath done for the Parliament these many years, or how many times, in our greatest distresses, we applying unto him, he hath refreshed our languishing expectations; he never failed us of comfort in our most unhappy distresses. I assure you his writings have kept up the spirits both of the soldiery, the honest people of this nation, and many of us Parliament men; and now at last, for a

---

199 Walter Strickland, an English political leader held in high esteem before and during Cromwell's Protectorate.
200 Robert Reynolds.

slip of his pen (if it were his) to be thus violent against him: I must tell you, I fear the consequence urged out of the book will prove effectually true. It is my counsel, to admonish him hereafter to be more wary, and for the present to dismiss him'.

Notwithstanding any thing that was spoken on my behalf, I was ordered to stand committed to the Serjeant at Arms. The messenger attached my person, said I was his prisoner. As he was carrying me away, he was called to bring me again. Oliver Cromwell, Lieutenant-General of the army, having never seen me, caused me to be produced again, where he stedfastly beheld me for a good space, and then I went with the messenger; but instantly a young clerk of that Committee asks the messenger what he did with me, where's the warrant? until that is signed you cannot seize Mr. Lilly, or shall. Will you have an action of false imprisonment against you? So I escaped that night, but next day obeyed the warrant. That night Oliver Cromwell went to Mr. R. my friend, and said, 'What never a man to take Lilly's cause in hand but yourself? None to take his part but you? He shall not be long there'. Hugh Peters spoke much in my behalf to the Committee; but they were resolved to lodge me in the Serjeant's custody. One Millington, a drunken member, was much my enemy; and so was Cawley and Chichester, a deformed fellow, unto whom I had done several courtesies.

First thirteen days I was a prisoner; and though every day of the Committee's sitting I had a petition to deliver, yet so many churlish Presbyterians still appeared, I could not get it accepted. The last day of the thirteen, Mr. Joseph Ash was made Chairman, unto whom my cause being related, he took my petition, and said I should be bailed in despite of them all, but desired I would procure as many friends as I could to be there. Sir Arthur Hazelrigg, and Major Salloway, a person of excellent parts, appeared for me, and many now of my old friends came in. After two whole hours arguing of my cause by Sir Arthur and Major Salloway, and other friends, the matter came to this point; I should be bailed, and a Committee nominated to examine the printer. The order of the Committee being brought afterwards to him who should be Chairman, he sent me word, do what I would, he would see all the knaves hanged, ere he would examine the printer. This is the truth of the story.

The 16th of February 1655, my second wife died; for whose death I shed no tears. I had five hundred pounds with her as a portion, but she and her poor relations spent me one thousand pounds. *Gloria Patri, & Filio, & Spiritui Sancto: sicut erat in principio & nunc, & semper, & in sæcula sæculorum.*[201] for the 20th of April 1655, these enemies of mine, viz. Parliament men, were turned out of doors by Oliver Cromwell.[202] A German doctor of physick being then in London, sent me this paper:

---

201 "Glory be to the Father, the Son, and the Holy Spirit: as it was in the beginning, and now, and for ever, and forever and ever."
202 Signaling the end of Rump Parliament, and the beginning of Cromwell's Protectorate.

Strophe Alcaica: Generoso Domino Gulielmo Lillio Astrologo, de dissoluto nuper Parliamento.

*Quod calculasti Sydere prævio,
Miles peregit numine conscio;
Gentis videmus nunc Senatum
Marte togaque gravi levatum.*[203]

In the time of my imprisonment, Mr. Rushworth[204] came to visit me, and told me, the army would do as much as I had predicted unto the Parliament.

In October 1654, I married the third wife, who is signified in my nativity by *Jupiter in Libra*; and she is so totally in her conditions, to my great comfort.

In 1655, I was indicted at Hicks's-Hall by a half-witted young woman.[205] Three several sessions she was neglected, and the Jury cast forth her bill; but the fourth

---

203 Roughly,

    In Alcaic Meter: Noble Lord William Lilly, Astrologer,
    On the Recently Dissolved Parliament.
    Whereas he first calculated the stars,
    The soldiers have carried out the Divine Will.
    The nation now sees the Senate,
    Mars and heavy gown lifted.

"Mars" here may be a clever planetary reference for war, and "heavy gown" a nod to the gowns worn by the members of Parliament. *(My thanks to Eric Purdue for assistance in this translation.)*

204 John Rushworth, English lawyer, politician and historian.

205 A copy of the indictment is available at the close of this autobiography, following the epitaphs written by English bishop George Smalridge.

time, they found it against me: I put in bail to traverse the indictment. The cause of the indictment was, for that I had given judgment upon stolen goods, and received two shillings and six-pence. – And this was said to be contrary unto an Act in King James's time made.[206]

This mad woman was put upon this action against me by two ministers,[207] who had framed for her a very ingenious speech, which she could speak without book, as she did the day of hearing the traverse.[208] She produced one woman, who told the court, a son of her's was run from her; that being in much affliction of mind for her loss, she repaired unto me to know what was become of him; that I told her he was gone for the Barbadoes, and she would hear of him within thirteen days; which, she said, she did.

A second woman made oath, that her husband being wanting two years, she repaired to me for advice: that I told her he was in Ireland, and would be at home such a time; and, said she, he did come home accordingly.[209]

I owned the taking of half a crown for my judgment of the theft; but said, I gave no other judgment, but that the goods would not be recovered, being that was all which was required of me: the party, before that, having

---

206 The Witchcraft Act. See note 49.

207 Likely Presbyterian ministers.

208 A traverse is a denial of something alleged by the opposition in legal proceedings.

209 Poor witnesses for the plaintiff to produce, as the two ladies have done little more than to identify Lilly as an effective and knowledgeable horary astrologer.

been with several astrologers, some affirming she should have her goods again, others gave contrary judgment, which made her come unto me for a final resolution.

At last my enemy began her before-made speech, and, without the least stumbling, pronounced it before the court; which ended, she had some queries put unto her, and then I spoke for myself, and produced my own *Introduction* into court, saying, that I had some years before emitted that book for the benefit of this and other nations; that it was allowed by authority, and had found good acceptance in both universities; that the study of astrology was lawful, and not contradicted by any scripture; that I neither had, or ever did, use any charms, sorceries, or inchantments related in the bill of indictment, &c.

She then related, that she had been several times with me, and that afterwards she could not rest a-nights, but was troubled with bears, lions, and tygers, &c. My counsel was the Recorder Green, who after he had answered all objections, concluded astrology was a lawful art.

'Mistress', said he, 'what colour was those beasts that you were so terrified with?'

'I never saw any', said she.

'How do you then know they were lions, tygers, or bears?' replied he. – 'This is an idle person, only fit for Bedlam'.[210] The Jury who went not from the bar,

---

[210] An alternative name for Bethlem Royal Hospital, an institution for the mentally unsound. Over time any such hospital became known as a bedlam.

brought in, No true Bill.[211]

There were many Presbyterian Justices much for her, and especially one Roberts, a busy fellow for the Parliament, who after his Majesty came in, had like to have lost life and fortune.

I had procured Justice Hooker to be there, who was the oracle of all the Justices of Peace in Middlesex.

There was nothing memorable after that happened unto me, until 1650, and the month of October, at what time Captain Owen Cox brought me over from his Majesty of Sweden, a gold chain and medal, worth about fifty pounds; the cause whereof was, that in the year 1657 and 1658, I had made honourable mention of him: the *Anglicus* of 1658 being translated into the language spoke at Hamburgh, printed and cried about the streets, as it is in London.

The occasion of my writing so honourably of his Majesty of Sweden was this: Sir Bolstrode Whitlock, Knight, upon the very time of Oliver's being made Protector, having made very noble articles betwixt Christina then Queen of Sweden,[212] and the English nation, was in his being at Stockholm visited frequently by Charles Gustavus,[213] unto whom Christina resigned during his abode,[214] and used with all manner of civility by him,

---

211 A "no bill" is a legal proceeding that dismisses a case and all related charges against a defendant when the prosecution is unable to produce sufficient evidence that the defendant has broken the law.

212 Christina was the Queen regent of Sweden, cousin of Charles X Gustavus.

213 The King of Sweden.

214 Christina abdicated the throne to Charles X Gustavus in 1654.

insomuch as some other Ambassadors took it ill, that they had not so much respect or equal: unto which he would reply, he would be kind where himself did find just cause of merit unto any. He were a great lover of our nation; but there were some other causes also moving my pen to be so liberal, viz. The great hopes I had of his prevailing, and of taking Copenhagen and Elsinore,[215] which, if he had lived, was hoped he might have accomplished; and had assuredly done, if Oliver the Protector had not so untimely died ere our fleet of ships returned; for Oliver sent the fleet on purpose to fight the Dutch; but dying, and the Parliament being restored, Sir Henry Vane,[216] who afterwards was beheaded, had order from the Council of State to give order to the fleet what to do now Oliver was dead, and themselves restored. Vane, out of state-policy, gave the Earl of Sandwich direction not to fight the Dutch. Captain Symons, who carried those letters, swore unto me, had he known the letters he carried had contained any such prohibition, he would have sunk both ship and letters. Oliver said, when the fleet was to go forth, 'That if God blessed his Majesty of Sweden with Copenhagen, the English were to have Elsinore as their share; which if once I have', saith Oliver, 'the English shall have the whole trade of the Baltick Sea: I will make the Dutch find another passage, except they will pay such customs as I shall impose'. Consider-

---

215 The Swedes were then in war with Denmark, but found difficulties in Copenhagen when the Dutch sent a relief of military support.

216 Henry Vane the Younger, politician, statesman and (briefly) colonial governor.

ing the advantages this would have been to our English, who can blame my pen for being liberal, thereby to have encouraged our famous and noble seamen, or for writing so honourably of the Swedish nation, who had most courteously treated my best of friends, Sir Bolstrode Whitlock, and by whose means, had the design taken effect, the English nation had been made happy with the most beneficial concern of all Christendom.[217] I shall conclude about Oliver the then Protector, with whom obliquely I had transactions by his son-in-law, Mr. Cleypool; and to speak truly of him, he sent one that waited upon him in his chamber, once in two or three days, to hear how it fared with me in my sessions business; but I never had of him, directly or indirectly, either pension, or any the least sum of money, or any gratuity during his whole Protectorship; this I protest to be true, by the name and in the name of the most holy God.

In 1653, before the dissolution of the Parliament, and that ere they had chosen any for their Ambassador into Sweden, Mr. Cleypool came unto me, demanding of me whom I thought fittest to send upon that embassy into Sweden: I nominated Sir B. Whitlock, who was chosen, and two or three days after Mr. Cleypool came again: 'I hope, Mr. Lilly, my father hath now pleased you: Your friend Sir B. Whitlock is to go for Sweden'. But since I have mentioned Oliver Cromwell, I will relate something of him, which perhaps no other pen can, or will

---

217 Lilly made many predictions of success for the Swedish King, the majority of which failed to actualize as the King fell to pneumonia in 1660.

OLIVER CROMWELL

From an Original Picture by Walker

mention. He was born of generous parents in Huntingdonshire, educated some time at the university of Cambridge: in his youth was wholly given to debauchery, quarrelling, drinking, &c. *quid non*;[218] having by those means wasted his patrimony, he was enforced to bethink himself of leaving England, and go to New-England: he had hired a passage in a ship, but ere she launched out for her voyage, a kinsman dieth, leaving him a considerable fortune; upon which he returns, pays his debts, became affected to religion; is elected in 1640 a member of Parliament, in 1642 made a Captain of horse under Sir Philip Stapleton, fought at Edge-Hill; after he was made a Colonel, then Lieutenant-General to the Earl of Manchester, who was one of the three Generals to fight the Earl of Newcastle and Prince Rupert at York: Ferdinando Lord Fairfax, and Earl Leven the Scot, were the other two for the Parliament: the last two thinking all had been lost at Marston-Moor fight,[219] Fairfax went into Cawood Castle,[220] giving all for lost: at twelve at night there came word of the Parliament's victory; Fairfax being then laid down upon a bed, there was not a candle in the castle, nor any fire: up riseth Lord Fairfax,

---

218 "... & what not."

219 A battle in the first part of the Civil War that appeared certain to end in favor of the Royalists. At the finish, Prince Rupert and his troops were, as Lilly explains, overcome, and Parliament took the victory.

220 Cawood was initially a Royalist bunker, then captured by the Parliament's troops, only to be recaptured by the Earl of Newcastle for the Royalists. Lord Fairfax recaptured it for its final occupation, using the facility as a camp for prisoners of war.

procures after some time, paper, ink, and candle, writes to Hull,[221] and other garrisons of the Parliament's, of the success, and then slept.

Leven the Scot asked the way to Tweed: the honour of that day's fight was given to Manchester, Sir Thomas Fairfax's brigade of horse, and Oliver Cromwell's iron sides; for Cromwell's horse, in those times, usually wore head-pieces, back and breast-plates of iron. After this victory Cromwell became gracious with the House of Commons, especially the Zealots, or Presbyterians, with whom at that time he especially joined; the name Independent, at that time, viz. 1644, being not so much spoken of.

There was some animosity at or before the fight, betwixt the Earl of Newcastle and Prince Rupert; for Newcastle being General of his Majesty's forces in the North, a person of valour, and well esteemed in those parts, took it not well to have a competitor in his concernments; for if the victory should fall on his Majesty's side, Prince Rupert's forces would attribute it unto their own General, viz. Rupert, and give him the glory thereof: but that it happened, Prince Rupert, in that day's fight, engaged the Parliament's forces too soon, and before the Earl of Newcastle could well come out of York with his army; by reason whereof, though Rupert had absolutely routed the Scots and the Lord Fairfax's forces; yet ere timely assistance could second his

---

221 Kingston upon Hull, a key Parliamentary garrison holding a large arsenal of weaponry and ammunition.

army, Sir Thomas Fairfax and Cromwell had put him to flight, and not long after all Newcastle's army. A most memorable action happened on that day. There was one entire regiment of foot belonging to Newcastle, called the Lambs, because they were all new cloathed in white woollen cloth, two or three days before the fight. This sole regiment, after the day was lost, having got into a small parcel of ground ditched in, and not of easy access of horse, would take no quarter; and by mere valour, for one whole hour, kept the troops of horse from entering amongst them at near push of pike: when the horse did enter, they would have no quarter, but fought it out till there was not thirty of them living; those whose hap it was to be beaten down upon the ground as the troopers came near them, though they could not rise for their wounds, yet were so desperate as to get either a pike or sword, or piece of them, and to gore the troopers' horses as they came over them, or passed by them. Captain Camby, then a trooper under Cromwell, and an actor, who was the third or fourth man that entered amongst them, protested, he never in all the fights he was in, met with such resolute brave fellows, or whom he pitied so much, and said, 'he saved two or three against their wills'.

After the fight, Manchester marched slowly southward, &c. but at last came with his army to Newbury fight; which ended, he came for London, and there he accuseth Cromwell, being his Lieutenant, to the Parliament, of disobedience, and not obeying his orders.

The House of Commons acquaint Cromwell herewith, and charge him, as he would answer it before God, that the day following he should give them a full account of Manchester's proceedings, and the cause and occasion of their difference, and of the reasons why Manchester did not timely move westward for the relief of Essex, then in the west, who was absolutely routed, inforced to fly, all his foot taken, and all his ordnance and train of artillery, only the horse escaping.

Cromwell the next day gave this account to Mr. Speaker in the House of Commons – by way of recrimination.

That after God had given them a successful victory at Marston over the King's forces, and that they had well refreshed their army, Manchester, by their order, did move southward, but with such slowness, that sometimes he would not march for three days together; sometimes he would lie still one day, then two days; whereupon he said, considering the Earl of Essex was in the west, with what success he then knew not, he moved Manchester several times to quicken his march to the west, for relief of Essex, if he were beaten, or to divert the King's forces from following of Essex; but he said Manchester still refused to make any haste; and that one day he said, 'If any man but yourself, Lieutenant, should so frequently trouble me, I would call him before a Council of War. We have beaten the King's forces in the north; if we should do so in the west, his Majesty is then undone: he hath many sons living; if any of them come to the Crown, as they well may, they will never forget us'. This Major Hammond, a man of honour, will justify as well as myself. After which he marched not at all, until he had order from the Committee to hasten westward, by reason of Essex's being lost in Cornwall, which then he did; and at Newbury fight, it is true, I refused to obey his directions and order: for this it was; his Majesty's horse being betwixt four and five thousand in a large common, in good order, he commands me, Mr. Speaker, to charge them; we having no way to come at them but through a narrow lane, where not above three horse could march abreast; whereby had I followed his order, we had been all cut off ere we could have got into any order. Mr. Speaker, (and then he wept; which he could do *toties quoties*[222]) I, considering that all the visible army you then had, was by this counsel in danger to be lost, refused thus to endanger the main strength, which now most of all consisted of those horse under my command, &c. – This his recrimination was well accepted by the House of Commons, who thereupon, and from that time, thought there was none of the House of Lords very fit to be entrusted with their future armies, but had then thoughts of making a commoner their General; which afterwards they did, and elected Sir Thomas Fairfax their General, and Cromwell Lieutenant-General; but it was next spring first. Upon Essex's being lost in Cornwall, I heard Serjeant Maynard say, 'If now the King haste to London we are undone, having no army to resist him'.

---

222 "On occasion" – i.e., at will.

His Majesty had many misfortunes ever attending him, during his abode at Oxford;[223] some by reason of that great animosity betwixt Prince Rupert and the Lord Digby, each endeavouring to cross one another; but the worst of all was by treachery of several officers under his command, and in his service; for the Parliament had in continual pay one Colonel of the King's Council of War; one Lieutenant-Colonel; one Captain; one Ensign; one or two Serjeants; several Corporals, who had constant pay, and duly paid them every month, according to the capacity of their officers and places, and yet none of these knew any thing of each other's being so employed.[224] There were several well-wishers unto the Parliament in Oxford, where each left his letter, putting it in at the hole of a glass-window, as he made water in the street. What was put in at the window in any of those houses, was the same day conveyed two miles off by some in the habit of town-gardeners, to the side of a ditch, where one or more were ever ready to give the intelligence to the next Parliament garrison: I was then familiar with all the spies that constantly went in and out to Oxford.

But once more to my own actions. I had, in 1652 and 1653 and 1654, much contention with Mr. Gatacre of Rotherhithe,[225] a man endued with all kind of learning,

---

223 During the Civil War, Charles I thought it wise to leave London to set up base in Oxford.

224 Parliament's spies, or those officers they had in their pockets, hence Lilly's admonition of the treachery in Oxford.

225 Thomas Gataker, son of Thomas Gatacre, an English clergyman and

and the ablest man of the whole synod of divines in the Oriental tongues.

The synod had concluded to make an exposition upon the bible; some undertook one book, some another. Gatacre fell upon *Jeremy*.[226] Upon making his exposition on the 2d verse of the 10th chapter,

'Learn not the way of the heathen, and be not dismayed at the signs of heaven, for the heathen are dismayed at them.'

In his *Annotations* thereupon, he makes a scandalous exposition; and in express terms, hints at me, repeating *verbatim*, ten or twelve times, an *Epistle* of mine in one of my former *Anglicus*.

The substance of my *Epistle* was, that I did conceive the good angels of God did first reveal astrology unto mankind, &c. but he in his *Annotations* calls me blind buzzard, &c.

Having now liberty of the press, and hearing the old man was very cholerick, I thought fit to raise it up – and only wrote – I referred my discourse then in hand to the discussion and judgment of sober persons, but not unto Thomas Wiseacre, for *Senes bis pueri*:[227] These very words begot the writing of forty-two sheets against myself and astrology. The next year I quibbled again in three or four lines against him, then he printed twenty-two sheets against me. I was persuaded by Dr. Gauden, late Bishop

---

theologian.
226 That is, Jeremiah.
227 "A twice-aged boy."

of Exeter, to let him alone; but in my next year's *Anglicus*, in August observations, I wrote, *Hâc in tumbâ jacet Presbyter & Nebulo*,[228] in which very month he died.[229]

Several divines applied themselves unto me, desiring me to forbear any further vexing of Mr. Gatacre; but all of them did as much condemn him of indiscretion, that in so sober a piece of work as that was, viz. in an *Annotation* upon a sacred text of scripture to particularize me and in that dirty language: they pitied him, that he had not better considered with himself ere he published it.[230]

Dean Owen of Christ's-Church in Oxford, also in his sermons had sharp invectives against me and astrology; I cried quittance with him, by urging Abbot Panormitan's judgment of astrology contrary to Owen's, and concluded, 'An Abbot was an ace above a Dean'.

One Mr. Nye of the assembly of divines, a Jesuitical Presbyterian, bleated forth his judgment publickly

---

228 "Here in this tomb lies a Presbyter and a knave."

229 In his introduction to *A Complete Refutation of Astrology* (1838), T. H. Croft Moody quotes the author of *Demonologia*, who said bitterly of this prophecy, "[Lilly] had the impudence to assert, that he had predicted Gatacre's death! But the truth is, it was an epitaph to the 'lodgings to let;' it stood empty, ready for the first passenger to inhabit. Had any other party of any eminence died in that month, it would have been as appositely applied to him. But Lilly was an exquisite rogue, and never at a fault" (xx). Moody's *Refutation* reports that Gataker died in 1694, which is clearly a typographical error – Gataker in fact died in 1654.

230 Much earlier than this miscalculation in judgment was Gataker's publication of *Of the Nature and Use of Lots* in 1619, a treatise that caused a number of his fellow clergymen to accuse him of enabling and/or normalizing a vice of gambling.

against me and astrology: to be quit with him, I urged Causinus the Jesuit's approbation of astrology,[231] and concluded, *Sic canibus catulos, &c.*[232]

In some time after the Dutch Ambassador being offended with some things in *Anglicus*,[233] presented a memorial to the Council of State, that *Merlinus Anglicus* might be considered, and the abuses against their nation examined; but his paper was not accepted of, or I any way molested.

In Oliver's Protectorship, I wrote freely and satyrical enough: he was now become Independant, and all the soldiery my friends; for when he was in Scotland, the day of one of their fights, a soldier stood with *Anglicus* in his hand; and as the several troops passed by him, 'Lo, hear what Lilly saith; you are in this month promised victory, fight it out, brave boys'; and then read that month's prediction.

I had long before predicted the downfall of Presbytery, as you (most honoured Sir) in the figure thereof, in my *Introduction*, may observe;[234] and it was upon this occasion. Sir Thomas Middleton of Chark Castle, enemy to Presbytery, seeing they much prevailed, being a member of the House, seriously demanded my judgment, if Presbytery should prevail, or not, in England? The figure

---

231 Nicolas Caussin was a devout French Jesuit and theologian who served as astrologer to the French royal court.

232 "Thus the dogs were but puppies."

233 For Lilly had much to say about the Dutch, very little of it being positive.

234 "If Presbytery shall stand?", figure and delineation in Lilly's *Christian Astrology*, 439–42.

printed in my *Introduction*, will best give you an account, long before it happened, of the sinking and failing of Presbytery; so will the second page of my *Hieroglyphicks*. Those men, to be serious, would preach well; but they were more lordly than Bishops, and usually, in their parishes, more tyrannical than the Great Turk.

OF THE YEAR 1660; THE ACTIONS WHEREOF, AS THEY WERE REMARKABLE IN ENGLAND, SO WERE THEY NO LESS MEMORABLE AS TO MY PARTICULAR FORTUNE AND PERSON

Upon the Lord General Monk's returning from Scotland with his army into England, suddenly after his coming to London, Richard Cromwell, the then Protector's, authority was laid aside, and the old Parliament restored; the Council of State sat as formerly. The first act they put the General upon was, to take down the city gates and portcullisses, an act which, the General said, was fitter for a Janizary[235] to do than for a General; yet he effected the commands received, and then lodged in the city with his army. The citizens took this pulling down of their gates so heinously, that one night the ruder sort of them procured all the rumps of beef, and other baggage, and publickly burnt them in the streets, in derision of the then Parliament, calling them that now sat,

---

235 Janissary, a member of an elite Turkish guard.

The Rump. This hurly-burly was managed as well by the General's soldiers as the citizens. The King's health[236] was publickly drank all over the city, to the confusion of the Parliament. The matter continued until midnight, or longer. The Council of State, sitting at White-Hall, had hereof no knowledge, until Sir Martin Noell,[237] a discreet citizen, came about nine at night, and then first informed them thereof. The Council could not believe it, until they had sent some ministers of their own, who affirmed the verity thereof. They were at a stand, and could not resolve what to do; at last Nevil Smith came, being one of them, and publickly protested there was but one way to regain their authority, and to be revenged of this affront, and to overthrow the Lord General Monk, whom they now perceived intended otherways than he had pretended; his council was, to take away Monk's commission, and to give a present commission to Major-General Lambert to be their General; which counsel of his, if they would take and put it speedily in execution, would put an end unto all the present mischiefs. The Council in general did all very well approve Nevil Smith's judgment; but presently up starts Sir Arthur Hazellrigg, and makes a sharp invective against Lambert, and concluded, he would rather perish under the King of Scot's power, than that Lambert should ever any more have command under the Parliament.

---

236 The exiled Charles II.

237 An English merchant.

The Lord General suddenly after brings in the long excluded Members to sit in Parliament, being persons of great judgment, and formerly enforced from sitting therein by the soldiery, and connivance of those who ſtiled themselves the godly part of the Parliament.[238] These honourable patriots presently voted his Majeſty's coming into England, and so he did in May 1660. But because Charles the Second, now (1667) King of England, Son of Charles the Firſt, grandchild to James the Firſt, King of Great Britany, was so miraculously reſtored, and so many hundreds of years since prophesied of by Ambrose Merlin, it will not be impertinent to mention the prophecies themselves, the rather because we have seen their verification.

AMBROSE MERLIN'S PROPHECY WROTE ABOUT 990 YEARS SINCE[239]

He calls King James, The Lion of Righteousness; and saith, when he died, or was dead, there would reign a noble White King; this was Charles the Firſt. The prophet discovers all his troubles, his flying up and down, his imprisonment, his death; and calls him Aquila. What concerns Charles the Second, is the subjeƈt of our discourse: in the Latin copy it is thus:

---

238 This is the same enforcement by soldiery that Lilly predicted in his 1652/3 *Anglicus*. His tone here is much more diplomatic and careful than it was in his almanac.

239 Discussed at length in Lilly's Prophecy of the *White King* (1644).

Deinde ab Austro veniet cum Sole super ligneos equos, & super spumantem inundationem maris, Pullus Aquilæ navigans in Britanniam.

Et applicans statim tunc altam domum Aquilæ sitiens, & cito aliam sitiet.

Deinde Pullus Aquilæ nidificabit in summa rupe totius Britanniæ: nec juvenis occidet, nec ad senem vivet.

This, in an old copy, is Englished thus:

'After then, shall come through the south with the sun, on horse of tree, and upon all waves of the sea, the Chicken of the Eagle, sailing into Britain, and arriving anon to the house of the Eagle, he shall shew fellowship to them beasts.

'After, the Chicken of the Eagle shall nestle in the highest rock of all Britain: nay, he shall nought be slain young; nay, he nought come old'.

Another Latin copy renders the last verse thus:

Deindè pullus Aquilæ nidificabit in summo rupium, nec juvenis occidetur, nec ad senium perveniet. There is after this, *percificato regno omnes occidet;* which is intended of those persons put to death, that sat as Judges upon his father's death.

THE VERIFICATION

His Majesty being in the Low-Countries when the Lord General had restored the secluded Members, the Parliament sent part of the Royal Navy to bring him for England, which they did in May 1660. Holland is East from England, so he came with the sun; but he landed at Dover, a port in the south part of England. Wooden-horses, are the English ships.

Tunc nidificabit in summo rupium.[240]

The Lord General, and most of the gentry in England, met him in Kent, and brought him unto London, then to White-hall.

Here, by the highest Rooch, (some write Rock,) is intended London, being the metropolis of all England.

Since which time, unto this very day I write this story, he hath reigned in England, and long may he do hereafter. 10th December, 1667.[241]

Had I leisure, I might verify the whole preceding part concerning King Charles. Much of the verification thereof is mentioned in my *Collection of Prophecies*, printed 1645. But his Majesty being then alive, I forbore much of that subject, not willing to give offence. I dedicated that book unto him; and, in the conclusion thereof, I advised his return unto Parliament, with these words, *Fac hoc & vives.*[242]

There was also a *Prophecy* printed 1588, in Greek characters, exactly decyphering the long troubles the English nation had from 1641 until 1660; and then it ended thus:

'And after that shall come a dreadful dead man, and with him a Royal G'. [it is Gamma in the Greek, intending C. in the Latin, being the third letter in the

---

240 "Then the next on top of the cliffs."

241 King Charles II reigned until his death by apoplexy in 1685.

242 "Do this, and you live."

alphabet,] 'of the best blood in the world, and he shall have the Crown, and shall set England on the right way, and put out all heresies'.

Monkery being extinguished above eighty or ninety years, and the Lord General's name being Monk, is the Dead Man. The Royal G. or C. is Charles the Second, who, for his extraction, may be said to be of the best blood in the world.

These two prophecies were not given vocally by the angels, but by inspection of the crystal in types and figures, or by apparition the circular way, where, at some distance, the angels appear, representing by forms, shapes, and creatures, what is demanded. It is very rare, yea, even in our days, for any operator or master to have the angels speak articulately; when they do speak, it is like the Irish, much in the throat.

What further concerns his Majesty, will more fully be evident about 1672 or 1674, or, at farthest, in 1676. And now unto my own actions in 1660.

In the first place, my fee-farm rents, being of the yearly value of one hundred and twenty pounds, were all lost by his Majesty's coming to his restoration: but I do say truly, the loss thereof did never trouble me, or did I repine thereat.

In June of that year, a new Parliament was called, whereunto I was unwillingly invited by two messengers of the Serjeant at Arms. The matter whereupon I was taken into custody was, to examine me concerning the person who cut off the King's head, viz. the late King's.[243]

Sir Daniel Harvey, of Surry, got the business moved against me in great displeasure, because, at the election of new knights for Surrey, I procured the whole town of Walton to stand, and give their voices for Sir Richard Onslow. The Committee to examine me, were Mr. Prinn, one Colonel King, and Mr. Richard Weston of Gray's-Inn.

God's providence appeared very much for me that day, for walking in Westminster-Hall, Mr. Richard Pennington, son to my old friend Mr. William Pennington, met me, and enquiring the cause of my being there, said no more, but walked up and down the hall, and related my kindness to his father unto very many Parliament men of Cheshire and Lancashire, Yorkshire, Cumberland, and those northern countries, who numerously came up into the Speaker's chamber, and bade me be of good comfort: at last he meets Mr. Weston, one of the three unto whom my matter was referred for examination, who told Mr. Pennington, that he came purposely to punish me; and would be bitter against me; but hearing it related, viz. my singular kindness and preservation of old Mr. Pennington's estate to the value of six or seven thousand pounds, 'I will do him all the good I can', says he. 'I thought he had never done any good; let me see him, and let him stand behind me where I sit': I did so. At my first appearance, many of the young

---

243 Lilly had occasionally boasted inside knowledge of the individual responsible for beheading the King.

members affronted me highly, and demanded several scurrilous questions. Mr. Weston held a paper before his mouth; bade me answer nobody but Mr. Prinn; I obeyed his command, and saved myself much trouble thereby; and when Mr. Prinn put any difficult or doubtful query unto me, Mr. Weston prompted me with a fit answer. At last, after almost one hour's tugging, I desired to be fully heard what I could say as to the person who cut Charles the First's head off. Liberty being given me to speak, I related what follows, viz.

That the next Sunday but one after Charles the First was beheaded, Robert Spavin, Secretary unto Lieutenant-General Cromwell at that time, invited himself to dine with me, and brought Anthony Peirson, and several others, along with him to dinner: that their principal discourse all dinner-time was only, who it was that beheaded the King; one said it was the common hangman; another, Hugh Peters; others also were nominated, but none concluded. Robert Spavin, so soon as dinner was done, took me by the hand, and carried me to the south window: saith he, 'These are all mistaken, they have not named the man that did the fact: it was Lieutenant-Colonel JOICE; I was in the room when he fitted himself for the work, stood behind him when he did it; when done, went in again with him: there is no man knows this but my master, viz. Cromwell, Commissary Ireton, and myself'. 'Doth not Mr. Rushworth know it?' said I. 'No, he doth not know it', saith Spavin. The same thing Spavin since had often related unto me when we were alone. Mr. Prinn did, with much civility, make a report hereof in the House; yet Norfolk the Serjeant, after my discharge, kept me two days longer in arreſt, purposely to get money of me. He had six pounds, and his Messenger forty shillings; and yet I was attached but upon Sunday, examined on Tuesday, and then discharged, though the covetous Serjeant detained me until Thursday. By means of a friend, I cried quittance with Norfolk, which friend was to pay him his salary at that time, and abated Norfolk three pounds, which we spent every penny at one dinner, without inviting the wretched Serjeant: but in the latter end of the year, when the King's Judges were arraigned at the Old-Bailey, Norfolk warned me to attend, believing I could give information concerning Hugh Peters. At the sessions I attended during its continuance, but was never called or examined. There I heard Harrison, Scott, Clement, Peters, Hacker, Scroop, and others of the King's Judges, and Cook the Sollicitor, who excellently defended himself; I say, I did hear what they could say for themselves, and after heard the sentence of condemnation pronounced againſt them by the incomparably modeſt and learned Judge Bridgman, now Lord Keeper of the Great Seal of England.

One would think my troubles for that year had been ended; but in January 1662, one Everard, a Juſtice of Peace in Weſtminſter, ere I was ſtirring, sent a Serjeant and thirty four musqueteers for me to White-Hall: he had twice that night seized about sixty persons, supposed fanaticks,[244] very despicable persons, many whereof were aged, some were water-bearers, and had been Parliament-soldiers; others, of ordinary callings: all these were guarded unto White-Hall, into a large room, until daylight, and then committed to the Gate-House; I was had into the guard-room, which I thought to be hell; some therein were sleeping, others swearing, others smoking tobacco. In the chimney of the room I believe there was two bushels of broken tobacco-pipes, almost half one load of ashes. Everard, about nine in the morning, comes, writes my mittimus[245] for the Gate-House, then shews it me: I must be contented. I desired no other courtesy, but that I might be privately carried unto the Gate-House by two soldiers; that was denied. Among the miserable crew of people, with a whole company of soldiers, I marched to prison, and there for three hours was in the open air upon the ground, where the common house of office came down. After three hours, I was advanced from this stinking place up the stairs, where there was on one side a company of rude swearing persons; on the other side many Quakers, who lovingly entertained me. As soon as I was fixed, I wrote to my old friend Sir Edward Walker, Garter King at Arms, who presently went to Mr. Secretary Nicholas, and acquainted him with my condition. He ordered Sir Edward to write to Everard to release me, unless he had any particular information

---

244 Witches, sorcerers, magicians, fortune-tellers, charlatans, etc.

245 A document commanding a jailer to safely transport a convict to a prison, or some other holding location.

against me, which he had not. He further said, it was not his Majesty's pleasure that any of his subjects should be thus had to prison without good cause shewed before. Upon receipt of Sir Edward's letter, Everard discharged me, I taking the oaths of allegiance and supremacy. This day's work cost me thirty-seven shillings. Afterwards Everard stood to be Burgess for Westminster; sent me to procure him voices. I returned answer, that of all men living he deserved no courtesy from me, nor should have any.

In this year 1660, I sued out my pardon under the Broad Seal of England, being so advised by good counsel, because there should be no obstruction; I passed as William Lilly, Citizen and Salter of London; it cost me thirteen pounds six shillings and eight pence.

There happened a verification of an astrological judgment of mine in this year, 1660, which, because it was predicted sixteen years before it came to pass, and the year expressly nominated, I thought fit to mention.

In page 111 of my *Prophetical Merlin*, upon three sextile Aspects of Saturn and Jupiter, made in 1659 and 1660, I wrote thus –

'This their friendly salutation comforts us in England, every man now possesses his own vineyard; our young youth grow up unto man's estate, and our old men live their full years; our nobles and gentlemen root again; our yeomanry, many years disconsolated, now take pleasure in their husbandry. The merchant sends out ships, and hath prosperous returns; the mechanick hath quick trading: here is almost a new world; new laws, new

Lords. Now my country of England shall shed no more tears, but rejoice with, and in the many blessings God gives or affords her annually'.

And in the same book, page 118, over-against the year 1660, you shall find, A bonny Scot acts his part.

The long Parliament would give Charles the Second no other title than King of Scots.

I also wrote to Sir Edward Walker, Kt. Garter King at Arms in 1659, he then being in Holland –

Tu, Dominusque vester videbitis Angliam, infra duos annos.[246] – For in 1662, his moon came by direction to the body of the sun.

But he came in upon the ascendant directed unto the trine of Sol and antiscion of Jupiter.

And happy it was for the nation he did come in, and long and prosperously may he reign amongst us.

In 1663 and 1664, I had along and tedious law-suit in Chancery, M.C. coming to quartile of Saturn; and the occasion of that suit, was concerning houses; and my enemy, though aged, had no beard, was really saturnine. We came unto a hearing Feb. 1664, before the Master of the Rolls, Sir Harbottle Grimston, where I had the victory, but no costs given me.

My adversary, not satisfied with that judgment, petitioned that most just and honourable man, the Lord Chancellor Hyde, for a re-hearing his cause before him.

It was granted, and the 13th June, 1664, my M.C. then directed to quartile of Venus and Sol. His Lordship most

---

246 "You will see the Lord of England, within the space of two years."

judiciously heard it with much attention, and when my adversary's counsel had urged those depositions which they had against me, his Lordship stood up, and said,

'Here is not one word against Mr. Lilly'. –

I replied, 'My Lord, I hope I shall have costs'.

'Very good reason', saith he; and so I had: and, at my departure out of court, put off his hat, and bid 'God be with you'.

This is the month of Dec. 1667, wherein, by misfortune, he is much traduced and highly persecuted by his enemies: is also retired, however not in the least questioned for any indirect judgment as Chancellor, in the Chancery; [but in other things he hath been very foul, as in the articles drawn up by the Parliament against him, it appears. Which articles I presume you have not seen, otherwise you would have been of another mind, A W] for there was never any person sat in that place, who executed justice with more uprightness, or judgment, or quickness for dispatch, than this very noble Lord. God, I hope, in mercy will preserve his person from his enemies, and in good time restore him unto all his honours again: from my soul I wish it, and hope I shall live to see it. Amen: *Fiat oh tu Deus justitiæ.*[247]

In 1663 and 1664, I was made churchwarden of Walton upon Thames, settling as well as I could the affairs of that distracted parish, upon my own charges; and upon my leaving the place, forgave them seven pounds odd money due unto me.

---

247 "So be it, oh thou art the God of justice."

In 1664, I had another law-suit with Captain Colborn, Lord of the manor of Esher, concerning the rights of the parish of Walton. He had newly purchased that manor, and having one hundred and fifty acres of ground, formerly park and wood ground lying in our parish, conceived, he had right of common in our parish of Walton: thereupon, he puts three hundred sheep upon the common; part whereof I impounded: he replevins[248] them, and gave me a declaration. I answered it. The trial was to be at the Assizes at Kingston in April 1664. When the day of trial came, he had not one witness in his cause, I had many; whereupon upon conference, and by mediation, he gave me eleven pounds for my charges sustained in that suit, whereof I returned him back again fifty shillings: forty shillings for himself, and ten shillings for the poor of the parish he lived in.

This I did at my own cost and charges, not one parishioner joining with me. I had now M.C. under quartile of Venus and Sol – both in my second, ergo, I got money by this thing, or suit. Sir Bolstrode Whitlock gave me counsel.

Now I come unto the year 1665, wherein that horrible and devouring plague so extreamly raged in the city of London. 27th of June 1665, I retired into the country to my wife and family, where since I have wholly continued, and so intend by permission of God. I had, before I came away, very many people of the poorer sort frequented my lodging, many whereof were so civil, as

---

248 A lawsuit to reclaim what was wrongfully taken.

when they brought waters, viz. urines, from infected people, they would stand purposely at a distance. I ordered those infected, and not like to die, cordials, and caused them to sweat, whereby many recovered. My landlord of the house was afraid of those poor people, I nothing at all. He was desirous I should be gone. He had four children: I took them with me into the country and provided for them. Six weeks after I departed, he, his wife, and man-servant died of the plague.

In *Monarchy or no Monarchy*, printed 1651, I had framed an Hieroglyphick, which you may see in page the 7th, representing a great sickness and mortality; wherein you may see the representation of people in their winding-sheets, persons digging graves and sepultures, coffins, &c. All this was performed by the more secret *Key of Astrology*, or *Prophetical Astrology*.

In 1666, happened that miraculous conflagration in the city of London, whereby in four days, the most part thereof was consumed by fire. In my *Monarchy or no Monarchy*, the next side after the coffins and pickaxes, there is a representation of a great city all in flames of fire. The memorial whereof some Parliament men remembering, thought fit to send for me before that Committee which then did sit, for examination of the causes of the fire; and whether there was no treachery or design in the business, his Majesty being then in war both with the French and Dutch. The summons to appear before that Committee was as followeth.

'*Monday, 22d October*, 1666.

'At the Committee appointed to enquire after the causes of the late fires:

'ORDERED,

'That Mr. Lilly do attend this Committee on Friday next, being the 25th of October, 1666, at two of the clock in the afternoon, in the Speaker's chamber; to answer such questions as shall be then and there asked him.

'ROBERT BROOKE'

By accident I was then in London, when the summons came unto me. I was timorous of Committees, being ever by some of them calumniated, upbraided, scorned, and derided. However I must and did appear; and let me never forget that great affection and care yourself (Oh most excellent and learned Esquire Ashmole) shewed unto me at that time. First, your affection in going along with me all that day; secondly, your great pains and care, in speaking unto many worthy Members of that Committee your acquaintance, that they should befriend me, and not permit me to be affronted, or have any disgraceful language cast upon me. I must seriously acknowledge the persuasions so prevailed with those generous souls, that I conceive there was never more civility used unto any than unto myself; and you know, there were no small number of Parliament men appeared, when they heard I was to be there.

Sir Robert Brooke spoke to this purpose:

'Mr. Lilly, This Committee thought fit to summon you to appear before them this day, to know, if you can say any thing as to the cause of the late fire, or whether there might be any design therein. You are called the rather hither, because in a book of your's, long since printed, you hinted some such thing by one of your hieroglyphics'. Unto which I replied,

'May it please your Honours,

'After the beheading of the late King, considering that in the three subsequent years the Parliament acted nothing which concerned the settlement of the nation in peace; and seeing the generality of people dissatisfied, the citizens of London discontented, the soldiery prone to mutiny, I was desirous, according to the best knowledge God had given me, to make enquiry by the art I studied, what might from that time happen unto the Parliament and nation in general. At last, having satisfied myself as well as I could, and perfected my judgment therein, I thought it most convenient to signify my intentions and conceptions thereof, in Forms, Shapes, Types, Hieroglyphicks, &c. without any commentary, that so my judgment might be concealed from the vulgar, and made manifest only unto the wise. I herein imitating the examples of many wise philosophers who had done the like'.

'Sir Robert', saith one, 'Lilly is yet *sub vestibulo*'.[249]

I proceeded further. Said I, 'Having found, Sir, that the city of London should be sadly afflicted with

---

249 "Under court."

a great plague, and not long after with an exorbitant fire, I framed these two hieroglyphics as represented in the book, which in effect have proved very true'.

'Did you foresee the year?' said one.

'I did not', said I, 'or was desirous: of that I made no scrutiny'. I proceeded –

'Now, Sir, whether there was any design of burning the city, or any employed to that purpose, I must deal ingenuously with you, that since the fire, I have taken much pains in the search thereof, but cannot or could not give myself any the least satisfaction therein. I conclude, that it was the only finger of God; but what instruments he used thereunto, I am ignorant'.

The Committee seemed well pleased with what I spoke, and dismissed me with great civility.

Since which time no memorable action hath happened unto me, my retirement impeding all concourse unto me.

I have many things more to communicate, which I shall do, as they offer themselves to memory.

In anno 1634, and 1635, I had much familiarity with John Hegenius, Doctor of Physick, a Dutchman, an excellent scholar and an able physician, not meanly versed in astrology. Unto him, for his great civility, I communicated the art of framing Sigils, Lamens, &c. and the use of the Mosaical Rods: – and we did create several Sigils to very good purpose. I gave him, the true key thereof, *viz.* instructed him of their forms, characters, words, and last of all, how to give them vivification, and what number or numbers were appropriated to every planet: *Cum multis aliis in libris veterum latentibus; aut perspicuè non intellectis.*[250]

I was well acquainted with the Speculator[251] of John a Windor, a scrivener,[252] sometimes living in Newbury. This Windor was club-fisted, wrote with a pen betwixt both his hands. I have seen many bonds and bills wrote by him. He was much given to debauchery, so that at some times the Dæmons would not appear to the Speculator; he would then suffumigate: sometimes, to vex the spirits, he would curse them, fumigate with contraries.[253] Upon his examination before Sir Henry Wallop, Kt. which I have seen, he said, he once visited Dr. Dee in Mortlack; and out of a book that lay in the window, he copied out that call which he used, when he invocated —

It was that — which near the beginning of it hath these words,

Per virtutem illorum qui invocant nomen tuum,
Hermeli — *mitte nobis tres Angelos, &c.*[254]

Windor had many good parts, but was a most lewd person: My master Wright knew him well, and having

---

250 "With many others, hidden in the books of the ancients, or not clearly understood."

251 Scryer, or someone who looks into a crystal ball for predictive purposes.

252 Someone who could read and write, particularly legal documents.

253 Offering a suffumigation contrary to the invoked spirit's nature.

254 "Through the power of those who call upon your name, Hermeli, send us the three angels."

dealing in those parts, made use of him as a scrivener.

Oliver Withers, servant to Sir H. Wallop, brought up John a Windor's examination unto London, purposely for me to peruse. This Withers was Mr. Fiske's scholar three years more or less, to learn aſtrology of him; but being never the wiser, Fiske brought him unto me: by shewing him but how to judge one figure, his eyes were opened: He made the Epiſtle before Dr. Neve's book, now in Mr. Sander's hands, was very learned in the Latin, Greek, and Hebrew tongues.

Having mentioned Dr. John Dee, I hold it not impertinent to speak something of him; but more especially of Edward Kelly's Speculator.

Dr. Dee himself was a Cambro Briton, educated in the university of Oxford, there took his degree of Doctor; afterwards for many years in search of the profounder ſtudies, travelled into foreign parts: to be serious, he was Queen Elizabeth's intelligencer, and had a salary for his maintenance from the Secretaries of State. He was a ready witted man, quick of apprehension, very learned, and of great judgment in the Latin and Greek tongues. He was a very great inveſtigator of the more secret Hermetical learning, a perfect aſtronomer, a curious aſtrologer, a serious geometrician; to speak truth, he was excellent in all kinds of learning.

With all this, he was the moſt ambitious person living, and moſt desirous of fame and renown, and was never so well pleased as when he heard himself ſtiled Moſt Excellent.

DR. JOHN DEE

*From an Original Picture in the
Ashmolean Museum, Oxford*

He was studious in chymistry,[255] and attained to good perfection therein; but his servant, or rather companion, Kelly,[256] out-went him, *viz.* about the Elixir or Philosopher's Stone; which neither Kelly or Dee attained by their own labour and industry. It was in this manner Kelly obtained it, as I had it related from an ancient minister, who knew the certainty thereof from an old English merchant, resident in Germany, at what time both Kelly and Dee were there.

Dee and Kelly being in the confines of the Emperor's dominions, in a city where resided many English merchants, with whom they had much familiarity, there happened an old Friar to come to Dr. Dee's lodging. Knocking at the door, Dee peeped down the stairs. 'Kelly', says he, 'tell the old man I am not at home'. Kelly did so. The Friar said, 'I will take another time to wait on him'. Some few days after, he came again. Dee ordered Kelly, if it were the same person, to deny him again. He did so; at which the Friar was very angry. 'Tell thy master I came to speak with him and to do him good, because he is a great scholar and famous; but now tell him, he put forth a book, and dedicated it to the Emperor: it is called *Monas Hierogliphicas*.[257] He understands it not. I wrote it myself, I came to instruct him therein, and in some other more profound things. Do thou,

---

255 Alchemy.

256 Edward Kelley.

257 The Hieroglyphic Monad is an esoteric symbol containing various elements of all planetary symbols, designed by John Dee. Dr. Dee wrote about the symbol is his book, *Monas Hieroglyphica* (1564).

Kelly, come along with me, I will make thee more famous than thy master Dee'.

Kelly was very apprehensive of what the Friar delivered, and thereupon suddenly retired from Dee, and wholly applied unto the Friar; and of him either had the Elixir ready made, or the perfect method of its preparation and making. The poor Friar lived a very short time after: whether he died a natural death, or was otherwise poisoned or made away by Kelly, the merchant, who related this, did not certainly know.

How Kelly died afterwards at Prague, you well know: he was born at Worcester, had been an apothecary. Not above thirty years since he had a sister lived in Worcester, who had some gold made by her brother's projection.

Dr. Dee died at Mortlack in Surrey, very poor, enforced many times to sell some book or other to buy his dinner with, as Dr. Napier of Linford, in Buckinghamshire, oft related, who knew him very well.

I have read over his book of *Conference with Spirits*, and thereby perceive many weaknesses in the manage of that way of Mosaical learning: but I conceive, the reason why he had not more plain resolutions, and more to the purpose, was, because Kelly was very vicious, unto whom the angels were not obedient, or willingly did declare the questions propounded; but I could give other reasons, but those are not for paper.

I was very familiar with one Sarah Skelhorn, who had been Speculatrix unto one Arthur Gauntlet[258] about

---

258 Seventeenth-century magician who maintained his own grimoire of magical spells, remedies and invocations.

Gray's-Inn-Lane, a very lewd fellow, professing physick. This Sarah had a perfect sight, and indeed the best eyes for that purpose I ever yet did see. Gauntlet's books, after he was dead, were sold, after I had perused them, to my scholar Humphreys: there were rare notions in them. This Sarah lived a long time, even until her death, with one Mrs. Stockman in the Isle of Purbeck, and died about sixteen years since. Her mistress one time being desirous to accompany her mother, the Lady Beconsfield, unto London, who lived twelve miles from her habitation, caused Sarah to inspect her crystal, to see if she, viz. her mother, was gone, yea or not: the angels appeared, and shewed her mother opening a trunk, and taking out a red waistcoat, whereby she perceived she was not gone. Next day she went to her mother's, and there, as she entered the chamber, she was opening a trunk, and had a red waistcoat in her hand. Sarah told me oft, the angels would for some years follow her, and appear in every room of the house, until she was weary of them.

This Sarah Skelhorn, her call unto the crystal began, *'Oh ye good angels, only and only'*, &c.

Ellen Evans, daughter of my tutor Evans, her call unto the crystal was this:

'O Micol,[259] *O tu Micol, regina pigmeorum veni, &c.'*[260]

---

259 Michal, the daughter of Saul, a biblical King of Israel, and wife to David, who according to New Testament genealogical records was an ancestor of Jesus Christ.

260 "O Michal, O Michal, Queen of Colors, come." An invocation of the Queen of Fairies.

EDWARD KELLY

*From a Print Prefaced to
"Dr. Dee's Book of Spirits" 1659*

Since I have related of the Queen of Fairies, I shall acquaint you, that it is not for every one, or every person, that these angelical creatures will appear unto, though they may say over the call, over and over, or indeed is it given to very many persons to endure their glorious aspects; even very many have failed just at that present when they are ready to manifest themselves; even persons otherwise of undaunted spirits and firm resolution, are herewith astonished, and tremble; as it happened not many years since with us. A very sober discreet person, of virtuous life and conversation, was beyond measure desirous to see something in this nature. He went with a friend into my Hurst Wood: the Queen of Fairies was invocated, a gentle murmuring wind came first; after that, amongst the hedges, a smart whirlwind; by and by a strong blast of wind blew upon the face of the friend, – and the Queen appearing in a most illustrious glory, 'No more, I beseech you', (quoth the friend): 'My heart fails; I am not able to endure longer'. Nor was he: his black curling hair rose up, and I believe a bullrush would have beat him to the ground:[261] he was soundly laughed at, &c.

Sir Robert Holborn, Knight, brought once unto me *Gladwell of Suffolk, who had formerly had sight and conference with Uriel and Raphael, but lost them both by carelessness; so that neither of them both would but

---

261 A bulrush is a large wetland plant, not particularly sturdy. Lilly's joke here is that the invocation surprised his friend to such a degree that even something as faint as a bulrush could have knocked him to the ground. "He was soundly laughed at, &c."

rarely appear, and then presently be gone, resolving nothing. He would have given me two hundred pounds to have assisted him for their recovery, but I am no such man. – Those glorious creatures, if well commanded, and well observed, do teach the master any thing he desires; *Amant secreta, fugiunt aperta.*[262] The Fairies love the southern side of hills, mountains, groves. – Neatness and cleanliness in apparel, a strict diet, and upright life, fervent prayers unto God, conduce much to the assistance of those who are curious these ways.

It hath been my happiness to meet with many rarities in my time unexpectedly. I had a sister lived in the Minories, in that very house where formerly had lived one Evans, not my tutor, but another far exceeding him in astrology, and all other occult learning, questioned for his life about 1612. I am sure it was when the present Earl of Manchester's father was Lord Chief Justice of England. He was found guilty by a peevish Jury: but petitioning King James by a Greek petition, as indeed he was an excellent Grecian; 'By my saul', said King James, 'this man shall not die; I think he is a better Grecian than any of my Bishops': so his life was spared, &c.

* Mr. Gilbert Wakering gave him his berril when he died; it was of the largeness of a good big orange, set in silver, with a cross on the top, and another on the handle; and round about engraved the names of these angels, Raphael, Gabriel, Uriel.

---

262 "They love to fly open secrets."

My sister's master when new modelling the house, broke up a window, under which were Evans's secret manuscripts,* and two moulds in brass; one of a man, the other of a woman. I bought the moulds and book for five shillings; the secrets were wrote in an imperfect Greek character; but after I found the vowels, all the rest were presently clear enough.

You see, most worthy Sir, I write freely; it is out of the sincerity of my affection, many things wrote by me having been more fit for a sepulture than a book: But,

Quo major est virorum præstantium, tui similim inopia; eo mihi charior est, & esse debet & amicitia tua: quam quidem omnibus officiis, & studiis, quæ a summa benevolentia possunt, perpetuò colam:[263] However, who study the curiosities before-named, if they are not very well versed in astrology, they shall rarely attain their desired ends. There was, in the late times of troubles, one Mortlack, who pretended unto Speculations, had a crystal, a call of Queen Mab, one of the Queen of Fairies; he deluded many thereby: at last I was brought into his company; he was desired to make invocation, he did so; nothing appeared, or would: three or four times in my company he was put upon to do the work, but

* From these manuscripts he gained his first knowledge.

---

263 Roughly, "What great scarcity are men like you, men of superior ability, and that is and must be dearer to me than your friendship; which, indeed, by all offices, and studies, can be carried along by the highest benevolence, and with constant worship."

NAPIER OF MERCHISTON

From a Rare Print by Delaram

could not; at last he said he could do nothing as long as I was in presence. I at last shewed him his error, but left him as I found him, a pretending ignoramus.

I may seem to some to write incredibilia; be it so, but knowing unto whom, and for whose only sake, I do write them, I am much comforted therewith, well knowing you are the most knowing man in these curiosities of any now living in England; and therefore it is my hope, these will be a present well-becoming you to accept.

Præclara omnia quam difficilia sint, his præsertim temporibus. (Celeberrimè Armiger,) non te fugit;[264] and therefore I will acquaint you with one memorable story related unto me by Mr. John Marr, an excellent mathematican and geometrician, whom I conceive you remember: he was servant to King James and Charles the First.

At first, when the Lord Napier, or Marchiston, made publick his Logarithms, Mr. Briggs, then reader of the astronomy lecture at Gresham-College in London, was so surprized with admiration of them, that he could have no quietness in himself, until he had seen that noble person the Lord Marchiston, whose only invention they were: he acquaints John Marr herewith, who went into Scotland before Mr. Briggs, purposely to be there when these two so learned persons should meet. Mr. Briggs appoints a certain day when to meet at Edinburgh: but failing thereof, the Lord Napier was doubtful he would

---

264 "How difficult are the most excellent things, especially in these times. (Most learned Esquire,) you cannot escape it."

not come. It happened one day as John Marr and the Lord Napier were speaking of Mr. Briggs; 'Ah, John', saith Marchiston, 'Mr. Briggs will not now come': at the very instant one knocks at the gate; John Marr hasted down, and it proved Mr. Briggs, to his great contentment. He brings Mr. Briggs up into my Lord's chamber, where almost one quarter of an hour was spent, each beholding the other almost with admiration, before one word was spoke: at last Mr. Briggs began.

'My Lord, I have undertaken this long journey purposely to see your person, and to know by what engine of wit or ingenuity you came first to think of this most excellent help unto astronomy, viz. the Logarithms; but, my Lord, being by you found out, I wonder no body else found it out before, when, now known, it is so easy'. He was nobly entertained by the Lord Napier, and every summer after that, during the Lord's being alive, this venerable man, Mr. Briggs, went purposely into Scotland to visit him; *Tempora nunc mutantur.*[265]

These two persons were worthy men in their time; and yet the one, viz. Lord Marchiston, was a great lover of astrology, but Briggs the most satirical man against it that hath been known: but the reason hereof I conceive was, that Briggs was a severe Presbyterian, and wholly conversant with persons of that judgment; whereas the Lord Marchiston was a general scholar, and deeply read in all divine and human histories: it is the same

---

265 "The times are changing now."

Marchiston who made that most serious and learned exposition upon the *Revelation of St. John*; which is the best that ever yet appeared in the world.

THUS FAR PROCEEDED MR. WILLIAM LILLY in setting down the account of his life, with some other things of note. Now shall be added something more which afterwards happened during his retirement at his house at Hersham, until his death.

He left London in the year 1665, (as he hath before noted) and betook himself to the study of physick; in which, having arrived at a competent degree of knowledge, assisted by diligent observation and practice, he desired his old friend, Mr. Ashmole, to obtain of his Grace Dr. Sheldon, then Lord Archbishop of Canterbury, a license for the practice of physick; which upon application to his Grace, and producing a testimonial (October 8, 1670,) under the hands of two physicians of the college in London, on Mr. Lilly's behalf, he most readily granted, in the manner following, viz.

'GILBERTUS providentia divina Cantuariensis Archiepiscopus totius Angliæ Primas & Metropolitanus, dilecto nobis in Christo GULIELMO LILLY in Medicinis Professori, salutem, gratiam, & benedictionem. Cum ex fide digna relatione acceperimus Te in arte sive facultate Medicinæ per non modicum tempus versatum fuisse, multisque de salute & sanitate corporis verè desperatis (Deo Omnipotente adjuvante) subvenisse, eosque sanasse, nec non in arte predicta multorum peritorum laudabili testimonio pro experientia, fidelitate, diligentia & industria tuis circa curas quas susceperis peragendas in hujusmodi Arte Medicinæ meritò commendatum esse, ad practicandum igitur & exercendum dictam Artem Medicinæ in, & per totam Provinciam nostram Cant' (Civitate Lond' & circuitu septem milliarum eidem prox' adjacen' tantummodo exceptis) ex causis prædictis & aliis nos in hac per te justè moventibus, præstito primitus per te juramento de agnoscendo Regiam suprema potestatem in causis ecclesiasticis & temporalibus ac de renunciando, refutando, & recusando omni, & omnimodæ jurisdictioni potestati, authoritati & superioritati foraneis juxta vim formam & effectum statui Parliamenti hujus inclyti Regni Angliæ in ea parte editi & provisi quantum nobis per statuta hujus Regni Angliæ liceat & non aliter neque alio modo te admittimus & approbamus, tibique Licentiam & Facultatem nostras in hâc parte, tenore præsentium quamdiu te benè & laudabiliter gesseris benignè concedimus & elargimur. In cujus rei testimonium sigillum (quo in hâc parte utimur) praesentibus apponi fecimus. Dat. undecimo die mensis Octobris, Anno Domini 1670. Nostræque translationis Anno Octavo.

Sigillum

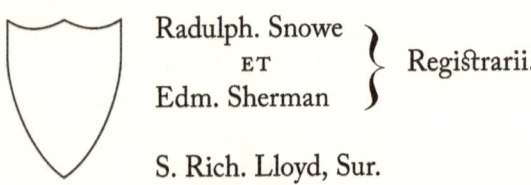

Radulph. Snowe
ET
Edm. Sherman
} Registrarii.

S. Rich. Lloyd, Sur.

'Vicarii in Spiritualibus Generalis per Provinciam Cantuariensem'.

Hereupon he began to practise more openly, and with good success; and every Saturday rode to Kingston, where the poorer sort flocked to him from several parts, and received much benefit by his advice and prescriptions, which he gave them freely, and without money. From those that were more able, he now and then received a shilling, and sometimes an half crown, if they offered it to him, otherwise he demanded nothing;[266] and, in truth, his charity towards poor people was very great, no less than the care and pains he took in considering and weighing their particular cases, and applying proper remedies to their infirmities, which gained him extraordinary credit and estimation.

He was of a strong constitution, and continued generally in good health, till the 16th of August 1674, when a violent humour discovered itself in red spots all over his body, with little pushes[267] in his head. This, in the winter (18 December) following, was seconded by a distemper whereof he fell sick, and was let blood in the left foot, a little above the ancle.

The 20th of December following, a humour descended from his head to his left side, from eight o'clock at

---

266 Parker shared, in his *Familiar to All*, a humorous anecdote found in a letter from Lilly to Ashmole regarding those impoverished clients he would see in his later years. One woman, 85 years of age, came to Lilly offering four measly pennies to keep her alive and well another twenty years. Lilly was convinced to accept her payment and "took her groat," fearing he would see no other clients that day. Lilly comments, "...but 2s came afterward. You see how I thrive" (247).

267 Boils, or pimples.

night till the next morning; and then staying a while in the calf of his leg, at length descended towards his toes, the anguish whereof put him into a fever. This humour fixed in two places on the top of his left foot (one in that where he was let blood two days before) which (upon application of pledgets[268]) growing ripe, they were [28 Dec.] lanced by Mr. Agar of Kingston, his apothecary (and no less a skilful Surgeon:) after which he began to be at ease, his fever abated, and within five months the cure was perfected.

The 7th of November 1675, he was taken with a violent fit of vomiting for some hours, to which a fever succeeded, that continued four months: this brought his body exceeding low, together with a dimness in his eyes, which after occasioned him to make use of Mr. Henry Coley, as his amanuensis,[269] to transcribe (from his dictates) his astrological judgments for the year 1677; but the monthly observations for that year, were written with his own hand some time before, though by this time he was grown very dim-sighted. His judgments and observations for the succeeding years, till his death, (so also for the year 1682,) were all composed by his directions, Mr. Coley coming to Hersham the beginning of every summer, and stayed there, till, by conference with him, he had dispatched them for the press; to whom, at these opportunities, he communicated his way of judgment, and other astrological arcanas.

---

268 Compresses.

269 A literary assistant that generally takes dictations.

In the beginning of the year 1681, he had a flux, which weakened him much, yet after some time his strength encreased; but now his sight was wholly taken from him, not having any glimmering as formerly.

He had dwelt many years at Hersham, where his charity and kindness to his poor neighbours was always great and hearty; and the 30th of May 1681, towards the evening, a dead palsy began to seize his left side. The second of June, towards evening, he took his bed, and then his tongue began to falter. The next day he became very dull and heavy: sometimes his senses began to fail him. Henceforward he took little or nothing, for his larinx swelled, and that impeded his swallowing.

The fourth of June, Mr. Ashmole went to visit him, and found he knew him, but spake little, and some of that scarce intelligible; for the palsy began now to seize upon his tongue.

The eighth of June he lay in a great agony, insomuch that the sweat followed drop after drop, which he bore with wonderful courage and patience (as indeed he did all his sickness) without complaint; and about three o'clock the next morning, he died, without any shew of trouble or pangs. Immediately before his breath went from him, he sneezed three times.

He had often, in his life-time, desired Mr. Ashmole to take care of his funeral, and now his widow desired the same: whereupon Mr. Ashmole obtained leave from Sir Mathew Andrews (who had the parsonage of Walton) to bury him in the chancel of that church.

The 10th of June, his corse[270] was brought thither, and received by the minister (in his surplice) at the Litch Gates, who, passing before the body into the church, read the first part of the *Office for the Burial of the Dead*. In the reading desk he said all the evening service, and after performed the rest of the office (as established by law) in the chancel, at the interment, which was about eight o'clock in the evening, on the left side of the communion table, Mr. Ashmole assisting at the laying him in his grave; whereupon afterwards [9 July 1681] he placed a fair black marble stone, (which cost him six pounds four shillings and six-pence) with this inscription following:

Ne Oblivione conteretur Urna
GULIELMI LILLII
ASTROLOGI PERITISSIMI,
QUI FATIS CESSIT
Quinto Idus Junii Anno Christi Juliano
M DC LXXXI.
Hoc Illi posuit amoris Monumentum
ELIAS ASHMOLE,
ARMIGER.

---

270 Archaic: corpse.

Shortly after his death, Mr. Ashmole bought his library of books of Mrs. Ruth Lilly, (his widow and executrix) for fifty pounds: he oft times, in his life-time, expressed, that if Mr. Ashmole would give that sum, he should have them.

The following Epitaphs (Latin and English) were made by George Smalridge, then a scholar at Westminster, after Student of Christ-Church in Oxford.

In Mortem Viri Doctissimi Domini Gulielmi Lilly, *Astrologi, nuper defuncti.*

Occidit atque suis annalibus addidit atram
   Astrologus, quâ non tristior ulla, diem
Pone triumphales, lugubris Luna, quadrigas;
   Sol mæstum piceâ nube reconde caput.
Illum, qui Phœbi scripsit, Phœbesq; labores
   Eclipsin docuit Stella maligna pati.
Invidia Astrorum cecidit, qui Sidera rexit
   Tanta erat in notas scandere cura domos.
Quod vidit, visum cupiit, potiturq; cupito
   Cœlo, & Sidereo fulget in orbe decus.
Scilicet hoc nobis prædixit ab ane Cometa,
   Et fati emicuit nuncia Stella tui
Fallentem vidi faciem gemuiq; videndo
   Illa fuit vati mortis imago suo,
Civilis timuere alii primordia belli
   Jejunam metuit plebs stupefata faniem
Non tantos tulerat bellumve famesve dolores:
   Auspiciis essent hæc relevanda tuis.
In cautam subitus plebem nunc opprimat ensis,
   Securos fati mors violenta trahat.
Nemo est qui videat moneatq; avertere fatum,
   Ars jacet in Domini funera mersa sui
Solus naturæ reservare arcana solebat,

Solus & ambigui solvere jura poti.
Lustrâsti erantes benè finâ mente Planeta
  Conspectum latuit stellata nulla tuum
Defessos oculos pensârunt lumina mentis
  Firesias oculis, mentibus Argus eras.
Cernere, Firesia, poteras ventura, sed, Arge,
  In fatum haud poteras sat vigil esse tuum
Sed vivit nomen semper cum sole vigebit,
  Immemor Astrologi non erit ulla dies
Sæcla canent laudes, quas si percurrere cones,
  Arte opus est, Stellas quâ numerare soles
Hæreat hoc carmen cinerum custodibus urnis,
  Hospes quod spargens marmora rore legat.
"Hic situs est, dignus nunquam cecidisse Propheta;
  Fatorum interpres fata inopina subit.
Versari æthereo dum vixit in orbe solebat:
  Nunc humilem jactat Terra superba virum.
Sed Coelum metitur adhuc resupinus in urnæ
  Vertitur in solitos palpebra clausa polos.
Huic busto invigilant solenni lampade Musaæ
  Perpetuo nubes imbre sepulchra rigant.
Ille oculis movit distantia Sidera nostris,
  Illam amota oculis traxit ad astra Deus."

An ELEGY *upon the Death of* WILLIAM LILLY, *the Astrologer.*

Our Prophet's gone; no longer may our ears
Be charm'd with musick of th' harmonious spheres.
Let sun and moon withdraw, leave gloomy night
To shew their NUNCIO's fate, who gave more light
To th' erring world, than all the feeble rays
Of sun or moon; taught us to know those days
Bright TITAN makes; follow'd the hasty sun
Through all his circuits; knew th' unconstant moon,
And more unconstant ebbings of the flood;
And what is most uncertain, th' factious brood,
Flowing in civil broils: by the heavens could date
The flux and reflux of our dubious state.
He saw the eclipse of sun, and change of moon
He saw, but seeing would not shun his own:
Eclips'd he was, that he might shine more bright,
And only chang'd to give a fuller light.
He having view'd the sky, and glorious train
Of gilded stars, scorn'd longer to remain
In earthly prisons: could he a village love,
Whom the twelve houses waited for above?
The grateful stars a heavenly mansion gave
T' his heavenly soul, nor could he live a slave
To mortal passions, whose immortal mind,
Whilst here on earth, was not to earth confin'd.
He must be gone, the stars had so decreed;
As he of them, so they of him, had need.
This message 'twas the blazing comet brought;

I saw the pale-fac'd ſtar, and seeing thought
(For we could guess, but only LILLY knew)
It did some glorious hero's fall foreshew:
A hero's fall'n, whose death, more than a war,
Or fire, deserv'd a comet: th' obsequious ſtar
Could do no less than his sad fate unfold,
Who had their risings, and their settings told.
Some thought a plague, and some a famine near;
Some wars from France, some fires at home did fear:
Nor did they fear too much: scarce kinder fate,
But plague of plagues befell th' unhappy ſtate
When LILLY died. Now swords may safely come
From France or Rome, fanaticks plot at home.
Now an unseen, and unexpected hand,
By guidance of ill ſtars, may hurt our land;
Unsafe, because secure, there's none to show
How England may avert the fatal blow.
He's dead, whose death the weeping clouds deplore,
I wish we did not owe to him that show'r
Which long expected was, and might have ſtill
Expected been, had not our nation's ill
Drawn from the heavens a sympathetic tear:
England hath cause a second drought to fear.
We have no second LILLY, who may die,
And by his death may make the heavens cry.
Then let your annals, COLEY, want this day,
Think every year leap-year; or if't muſt ſtay,
Cloath it in black; let a sad note ſtand by,
And ſtigmatize it to poſterity.

Here follows the Copy of an Indictment filed against Mr. Lilly, for which see page 127 of his Life.

The jurors for the Lord Protector of the commonwealth of England, Scotland, and Ireland, &c. upon their oaths do present, that William Lilly, late of the Parish of St. Clements Danes, in the County of Middlesex, Gent. not having the fear of God before his eyes, but being moved and seduced by the instigation of the devil, the 10th day of July, in the Year of our Lord, 1654, at the Parish aforesaid, in the County aforesaid, wickedly, unlawfully, and deceitfully, did take upon him, the said William Lilly, by inchantment, charm, and sorcery, to tell and declare to one Anne East, the wife of Alexander East, where ten waistcoats, of the value of five pounds, of the goods and chattels of the said Alexander East, then lately before lost and stolen from the said Alexander East, should be found and become; and two shilling and sixpence in monies numbred, of the monies of the said Alexander, from the said Anne East, then and there unlawfully and deceitfully, he, the said William Lilly, did take, receive, and had, to tell and declare to her the said Anne, where the said goods, so lost and stolen as aforesaid, should be found and become: And also that he, the said William Lilly, on the said tenth day of July, in the Year of our Lord, 1654, and divers other days and times, as well before as afterwards, at the said Parish aforesaid, in the County aforesaid, unlawfully and deceitfully did take upon him, the said William Lilly, by inchantment, charm, and sorcery, to tell and declare to divers other persons, to the said jurors, yet unknown, where divers goods, chattels, and things of the said persons yet unknown, there lately before loſt and ſtolen from the said persons yet unknown, should be found and become; and divers sums of monies of the said persons yet unknown, then and there unlawfully and deceitfully, he the said William Lilly did take, receive, and had, to tell and declare to the said persons yet unknown, where their goods, chattels, and things, so loſt and ſtolen, as aforesaid, should be found and become, in contempt of the laws of England, to the great damage and deceit of the said Alexander and Anne, and of the said other persons yet unknown, to the evil and pernicious example of all others in the like case offending, againſt the form of the ſtatute in this case made and provided, and againſt the publick peace, &c.

Anne Eaſt,
Emme Spencer,
Jane Gold,
Katherme Roberts,
Susannah Hulinge.

Butler's Character of WILLIAM LILLY.

* * * * *

* "A cunning man, hight SIDROPHEL.
That deals in destiny's dark counsels,
And sage opinions of the moon sells;
To whom all people, far and near,
On deep importances repair;
When brass and pewter hap to stray,
And linen slinks out of the way:

* *A cunning man, hight* SIDROPHEL. 'William Lilly, the famous astrologer of those times, who in his yearly almanacks foretold victories for the parliament with as much certainty as the Preachers did in their sermons; and all or most part of what is ascribed to him by the Poet, the reader will find verified in his "Letter," (if we may believe it) wrote by himself to Elias Ashmole, Esq'. For further curious information respecting William Lilly, the reader may consult *Dr. Grey's Notes to Hudibras*, vol. ii. page 163, &c. Edition 1819, in 3 vols, 8vo.

When geese and pullen are seduc'd,
And sows of sucking pigs are chous'd:
When cattle feel indisposition,
And need th' opinion of physician;
When murrain reigns in hogs or sheep,
And chickens languish of the pip;
When yeast and outward means do fail,
And have no power to work on ale;
When butter does refuse to come,
And love proves cross and humoursome;
To him with questions and with urine,
They for discov'ry flock, or curing.

* * * * *

He had been long t'wards mathematics,
Opticks, philosophy, and staticks,
Magick, horoscopy, astrology,
And was old dog at physiology:
But, as a dog that turns the spit,
Bestirs himself, and plies his feet
To climb the wheel, but all in vain,
His own weight brings him down again;
And still he's in the self-same place,
Where at his setting out he was:
So, in the circle of the arts,
Did he advance his nat'ral parts:
Till falling back still, for retreat,
He fell to juggle, cant, and cheat:
For as those fowls that live in water

Are never wet, he did but smatter:
Whate'er he labour'd to appear,
His underſtanding ſtill was clear,
Yet none a deeper knowledge boaſted,
Since old Hodge Bacon, and Bob Groſted,

* * * * *

Do not our great *Reformers* use
This SIDROPHEL to forebode news?
To write of victories next year,
And caſtles taken yet i'th' air?
Of battles fought at sea, and ships
Sunk, two years hence, the laſt eclipse?
A total o'er throw giv'n the KING
In Cornwall, horse and foot, next spring?
And has not he point-blank foretold
Whatso'er the *Close Committee* would?
Made Mars and Saturn for the *cause*,
The Moon for *fundamental laws*;
The Ram, the Bull, the Goat, declare
Againſt the *Book of Common Prayer*;
The Scorpion take the *Proteſtation*,
And Bear engage for Reformation;
Made all the *royal ſtars* recant,
Compound, and take the covenant."

THE END

BIBLIOGRAPHY

Albertus Magnus, "Speculum Astronomiae" in *The Speculum Astronomiae and Its Enigma – Astrology, Theology and Science in Albertus Magnus and His Contemporaries*, ed. Robert S. Cohen. Dordrecht: Kluwer Academic Publishers, 1992.

Appleby, Derek. *Horary Astrology: The Art of Astrological Divination*. Bel Air, MD: Astrology Classics, 2005.

Aquinas, Thomas. *The Summa Theologica*. New York: Benziger Bros, 1947.

Ashmole, Elias. *The History of the Most Noble Order of the Garter*. London, 1715.

Barclay, Olivia. *Horary Astrology Rediscovered*. West Chester, PA: Whitford Press, 1990.

Campbell, Jane. *The Retrospective Review (1820-1828) and the Revival of Seventeenth Century Poetry*. Waterloo, ON: Wilfrid Laurier University Press, 1974.

Cook, Judith. *Dr. Simon Forman: A Most Notorious Physician*. London, 2001.

Curry, Patrick. *Prophecy and Power: Astrology in Early Modern England*. Princeton, NJ: Princeton University Press, 1989.

Cust, Richard. *Charles I: A Political Life*. Harlow, UK: Pearson Longman, 2005.

Dawson, John S. "A Time to Die: William Lilly and the Execution of Charles I." *The Astrological Journal*, March/April 2007.

de Vore, Nicholas. *Encyclopedia of Astrology*. Bel Air, MD: Astrology Classics, 2005.

Dee, John. *Monas Hieroglyphica*, Kessinger Publishing Co., 2003.

deFord, Miriam Allen. *The Overbury Affair: the murder trial that rocket the court of King James I*. Philadelphia: Avon Book Division, 1960.

Fox, John. *The King's Smuggler: Jane Whorwood, Secret Agent to Charles I*. The History Press, 2011.

Gadbury, John. *Collectio Geniturarum: Or, a Collection of Nativities, in CL Genitures; Viz. Princely, Prelatical, Causidical, Physical, Mercatorial, Mathematical, Of Short Life, Of Twins, & c. With Many Useful Observations on them, Both Historical and Astrological. Being of Practical Concernment unto Philosophers, Physitians, Astronomers, Astrologers, And others that are Friends unto Urania*. London: 1662.

Gregg, Pauline. *King Charles I*. London: J. M. Dent, 1981.

Houlding, Deborah. *The Houses: Temples of the Sky*. Bournemouth, UK: The Wessex Astrologer Ltd., 2006.

Houlding, Deborah. "An Introduction to Horary Astrology, Part I: Considerations before Study and Cautionary Tales from History," *The Mountain Astrologer* 165, October, 2012.

Jacob, Giles. *A new law-dictionary containing the interpretation and definition of words and terms used in the law etc*. London, 1729.

Kieckhefer, Richard. *Magic in the Middle Ages*. Cambridge: Cambridge University Press, 2000.

Lilly, William, *England's Prophetical Merlin*. London, 1644.
———. *A Prophecy of the White King*. London, 1644.
———. *Supernatural Sights and Apparitions*. 1644.
———. *The Starry Messenger*. London, 1645.
———. *Christian Astrology* (1647). Regulus edition, 1985.
———. *Monarchy or No Monarchy in England*. London, 1651.
———. *Merlinus Anglicus*. London, 1652/3.
Moody, T. H. Croft. *A Complete Refutation of Astrology*. London, 1838.
Parker, Derek. *Familiar to All: William Lilly and Astrology in the Seventeenth Century*. London: Jonathan Cape Ltd., 1975.
Rudhyar, Dane. *The Practice of Astrology*. Stanwood, WA: Sabian Publishing Society, 1969.
Saunders, Richard. *The Astrological Judgement and Practice of Physick*. London: 1677.
Sharpe, Kevin. *The Personal Rule of Charles I*. New Haven & London: Yale University Press, 1912.
Sibly, Ebenezer. *The New and Complete Illustration of the Celestial Science of Astrology*. London: 1817.
Stockinger, Peter and Sue Ward, eds., *William Lilly: The Last Magician. Astrologer & Adept*. Oxford: Mandrake of Oxford, 2014.
Toohey, Sue. "And let them be for signs: Albertus Magnus & Prognostication by the Stars," 2006; http://www.skyscript.co.uk/magnus.html.
Wordsworth, Christopher, for the Church of England. *The Manner of the Coronation of King Charles the First of England at Westminster, 2 Feb. 1626*, London: Harrison and Sons, 1892.

SCRIBE SANGUINE
QUIA SANGUIS SPIRITUS

RUBEDO PRESS
AUCKLAND · SEATTLE · MMXV

www.ingramcontent.com/pod-product-compliance
Lightning Source LLC
Chambersburg PA
CBHW021432080526
44588CB00009B/504